# EMPTY CAGES

## KEYS TO FINDING FREEDOM

BY JESS BASSON

ISBN Paperback: 978–0–620–96697–9
ISBN: eBook: 978–0–620–96698–6

Illustrator: Jordan Gerber
Book Designer: Ashleigh-Jade Gouws

Printed and bound in South Africa by: Novus Printers
Second Edition, 2022

First Published by Jessica-Anne Basson 2021
Durban, South Africa
www.jessbasson.com

Jess Basson lives in Westbrook on the east coast of South Africa, with her husband Tom and their two wildlings, William and Luke. She loves gardening, her cats, walking on the beach, reading novels and procrasti-napping. She holds a Bachelor of Commerce in Marketing and Management from the University of KwaZulu Natal, South Africa, and a MA in Vocational Studies (Cum Laude) from Tabor College, Australia. As a speaker, coach, pastor, facilitator and writer, Jess wears many hats but her passion is to share life-transforming ideas.

www.jessbasson.com | @jessbasson

BOOK DESIGNER

Ashleigh-Jade was born a creative. She is a Design Thinker and Passionate Problem Solver to the core. She has a BA Honours degree in Digital Media, and a Master of Arts in Communication Design from Falmouth University in the UK.

www.coracreative.co | @coracreative.co

ILLUSTRATOR

Jordan lives on the North Coast of South Africa with her husband Jean and their daughter, Summer Rae. She's a lover of books, pasteries and the beach. Graphic Design and Illustrations are where her passions lie.

info@saintandivy.com | @saintandivy

"A witty and relatable guide to approaching the trials you face. A definite recommendation for my patients."

*- Candice Langford, Pelvic and Sexual Health Physiotherapist*

"Jess is so real, raw, candid and funny as she shares her story of self awareness, courage and deep joy that I could in so many parts relate to. *Empty Cages* tackles the stigma, anxiety and shame around mental health, motherhood and the relationship with self. Jess' voice is a gift to our collective sisterhood, being vulnerable and sharing our stories is such a powerful way of connecting us as we rise together."

*– Jane Linley-Thomas, Radio Presenter*

"*Empty Cages* had me captivated. Throughout each chapter I had moments of smiling, tearing up, and all too often wondering if Jess was either reading my mind or speaking directly to me. This book is a beautiful guide to freedom, and one I believe every woman should read to help get her wings back."

*– Shan Fourie, Digital Creator*

"As a writer and someone who truly appreciates the power of the written word, this book is a treasure to behold. Jess uses her vulnerability, personal experience and humour to educate, enlighten and equip us all for a world where ADHD exists and is grossly misunderstood. I have so enjoyed watching *Empty Cages* come to life and I know that it will set so many free to be their true and authentic selves."

*– Tes Jahnig, Pastor, Writer and Speaker*

"The journey to freedom from our own negative self-beliefs can be a hard one, but Jess has used her wit and candor to provide us with an experienced companion that will hold our hand, laugh with us and cry with us along the way."

*– Terence Mentor, Parenting Activist, Speaker and Blogger*

"*Empty Cages* is life-giving. It speaks to the vulnerable self that is often tucked so deeply inside of us that we forget the life it holds. Jess, through her amusing vulnerability, has written a gem of a book that will not only unlock many of our cages but guide us in stepping out of them into freedom, too."

***– Caitlyn de Beer, Author and Speaker***

"I laughed, I cried, but most of all, I related. An honest, light-hearted account of a woman finding the keys to her cages, with the hopes that you do too. As easy a read as a coffee date with a dear friend, I could hear Jess's energy in every word of *Empty Cages*."

***– Shaaista Kathree, Digital Creator***

"This book is fun, authentic, helpful and wise. Jess invites you to follow her into freedom by candidly introducing you to your captor. Spoiler alert: it's you!"

***– Jaci Mun-Gavin, Pastor and Author***

"Jess is brilliant, original and astonishingly funny. Finding solutions is so much easier when you know how to describe the actual problem. In this book, and all her work, Jess captures each challenge she's encountered with such honesty and humour that you won't help but journey with her on every page as she shares insightful keys to help you discover freedom."

***– Nande Boss, Business Leader***

"*Empty Cages* is a brave, relatable and relevant memoir. As a mom of three, I found myself in her pages and I just know that her story-driven life learnings will resonate with readers. Get ready to be nudged out of your cage with hands-on strategies and a healthy dose of humour!"

***– Julie Kynaston, Blogger and Digital Creator***

Whilst words are usually easy for me to find,
the ones that adequately express my love and gratitude
for my family continue to elude me.

This book is dedicated to:

***Mark and Christine van Straaten,***
for parenting me with wisdom, grace and acceptance.

***Tom Basson,***
for parenting our children with character, conviction and vision.

***William and Luke Basson,***
for teaching me to parent with humour, courage and kindness.

# PREFACE

Why should you read this book? I'd like you to imagine that you and I are seated next to each other at a posh dinner party, one where you have your name printed in a fancy font on a luxurious card, and they serve you each course at your seat, and you maybe had to buy some new shoes to be smart enough. We'd start off chatting casually, some light laughter and witty banter. By the end of the starter course, you'd be eyeing me thoughtfully and nodding to yourself, "I like this woman. I feel like she just understands me. Like, she just gets it. Also, such great shoes."

Then you'd start drifting off into thought, wondering what exactly it is that your new friend understands, but you'd be interrupted by the main course being served. As the rest of the table is buzzing back and forth, we'd slowly fade them out and grow more engrossed in our own conversation. We'd unpack interesting ideas and confess some questions we'd been wrestling with and then suddenly, something would happen. We'd look knowingly at each other because we'd realise – we've both been there.

We've struggled to find our way past our self-doubt and our disappointments. We've both lost our way a little bit, and we wonder what happened to that other version of our Self. The one that used to have exciting dreams for the future, used to feel confident and unafraid. We've both felt stuck, trapped, locked in a cage – only you don't know what your cage actually is or how to break free. Because you miss the old Self – the one before the kids, or the breakup, or the pandemic. Maybe you don't even know when your Before became an After – all you know is you haven't always been this way. You miss feeling like you're enough, like you're loved as you are, like you've got something inside of you that the world needs. You miss having the energy to live like you believe that.

As we share the knowledge that we've both been there, there'd be a pause. I would conspiratorially lean over, look you in the eye and I would tell you…

"It doesn't have to be like this. You were not made to be stuck in a cage. You were made to soar. You were made to flourish, to be free, to know who you are, and then go live like you believe it."

And then dessert would come on a silver tray, and it would be the most delicious dark chocolate brownie with a rosewater-vanilla gelato, and all conversation would grind to a halt.

Now, the chances of you experiencing this lavish dinner with a gloriously interesting and fun-loving kindred spirit who has great shoes sitting next to you, and then launching together into a journey of self-discovery and freedom are slim to none because I never get invited to these kinds of events.

But that, dear new friend, is why you need to read this book. Because I actually do know what it's like to feel stuck. I know what it's like to get out. And I want to help you do the same.

I'm inviting you to join me on the journey. The three parts of this book are sections of the pathway I've walked down, and are signposted as:

Part I: Beautiful Rowdy Prisoners
Part II: Dropping Keys
Part III: Empty Cages

The first section is for all the beautiful, rowdy prisoners. It's the story of how I found myself feeling so small, but not knowing why. If I was going to get out, I needed to find a name for my cage. Going back to my childhood, navigating motherhood and working towards a more healthy mental state revealed what my cage was. What is yours? As you travel back with me, you will learn how to find the clues to your own cage, and discover what locked you up somewhere on life's journey.

The second section is where you'll find the keys that are dropped along the way. I found them with a lot of wandering and wondering through motherhood, family, friendship and spirituality. So I've collected the moments and stories where I discovered each key, and I've bundled them together into a set so that you can use them, too. This set of keys are like those skeleton keys that international spies have – they work on every door, no matter whose it is.

Finally, I'll share with you a little glimpse of life outside of an empty cage. I'll help you find the inspiration and vision to keep flying free, and maybe even higher, brighter, further and bolder than you thought you could.

And when you're done with this book, promise me that you'll go spoil yourself with the most delicious chocolate brownie and ice cream you can find, take a photo, tag me online, and we can be friends forever.

Jess Basson
Westbrook
September 2021

www.jessbasson.com
@jessbasson

# EMPTY CAGES

# CONTENTS

# PART I
## BEAUTIFUL ROWDY PRISONERS

# CHAPTER ONE
## LAZY, HAZY AND CRAZY

We were driving back from our weekly dinner, heading home after half-price sushi and red wine. I still remember the section of the highway we were on as we left the little Chinese restaurant we'd been frequenting for over a decade of date nights on a Thursday. It was one of those heavy, humid evenings in Durban where the air is so thick with sea-spray that the yellow street lamps glow orange in the dark – balmy and warm, muggy and hot.

"What happened to me?" I wondered out loud to my husband as we cruised past the neighbourhood I'd grown up in. "I feel like I used to be such an ambitious, excited person. I feel like I've settled for smallness somewhere."

Once spoken out loud, that question followed me around like a desperately loyal little puppy clamouring for my attention. No ball I kicked to distract it could make it scamper off. Instead, it sat at my feet until I reluctantly picked it up and pulled it close.

What ***had*** happened to me?

My twenties and thirties had been filled with the usual changes. Growing up and moving around, changing seasons and changing my mind. Mostly, though, motherhood happened to me.

At first, it closed in on me.
And then, it unlocked the lid.

Andy Stanley says about parenting that
"The days are long but the years are short."

This is a story about the long days. Not my children's, but mine. The long days in the beginning when there haven't been enough years to make them feel short yet. The long days that unraveled me, and then the years that put me back together.

Nothing could have prepared me for motherhood – the love, the laughter and absolute wildness of our two boys.

First, our spirited, strong, hilarious little boy named William, came along. Two years later, he was followed by his delightful, warm and fun-loving brother, Luke. These two kids are rare gems of vivacity in a world that is filled with cautionary fear and a search for safety. Knowing where they come from in both nature and nurture, it's not surprising that these brothers take on life with all the adventure and courage that their little bodies can hold. They live voraciously, and to be honest, sometimes viciously, depending on how hungry or tired they are.

Someone once told me that boys are like dogs – you have to run them every day or they will break the furniture and dig up the garden. Someone was right.

William was a climber from the start. He climbed out of cots, up tables, over countertops, into trees, and along walls. In many ways, as our first born, he introduced us to the method of parenting we were going to use. It soon became evident that it was both exhausting and ridiculous to keep fetching him out of high places or pulling him away from the top of the jungle gym. Instead, I just decided to teach him myself how to do it properly.

I climbed into trees with him, showing him the difference between thick branches and thin branches, boughs that moved and ones that stayed still. If I couldn't keep him out of danger, I'd try to give him the skills to take on danger wisely.

Looking back, I realise this became a metaphor for our parenting.

Don't try to keep them safe. Teach them to be smart.

Yes, we've made a few visits to the emergency room for concussions and stitches, but I wouldn't trade that in for tentative, nervous living. Also, a scar tells a great story, especially when the story is that a wooden sword you tied onto a branch fell out of the tree and onto your head while you were jumping on the trampoline.

Early motherhood was when many gifts arrived in my life. At the time, these gifts were wrapped in fatigue and pureed food and days that go on for so long but you still can't remember what happened in them. Parenting will bring out the best and the worst in you. They're the flip side of the same coin.

I didn't have a clue about most mothering things, but the one that really caught me off guard was the undoing and putting back together that happened along the way.

I discovered that, while I was the fun mom who was up for spontaneous adventure, I was also the mom who dropped her kids off at school the day before the new term started. Twice. I learnt I was the mom who could happily set aside all the chores and sit with them on the floor, playing Lego for hours. I was, however, also the mom who never knew what they were meant to bring to school on Valentine's Day. I built forts in the garden with them, and lost all the forms that were meant to be returned to school with my signature on them. Parenting revealed that I was the mom who made up the most fantastic, hilarious stories, and was sometimes the only one who could make the toddler stop crying, because he was laughing instead. I'm also that mom who is on her third wedding ring. To be clear, the husband is still Tom, the same gorgeous, clever man I married at the age of twenty-two, but yes. Third wedding ring. I'm not going into details except to say that one involved getting the dog x-rayed, digging through poop for two weeks and getting one of those metal detector guys to walk through the garden.

I didn't know why I was like this, so I just made the reasons up. My forgetfulness, my scatter-brained diary, my inability to know where my sunglasses, keys and cellphone were at any given moment were annoying. Annoying but cloying, accumulating into labels that started to encircle me more fixedly. I lived inside these repetitive dynamics every day, unable to escape the frustrations they brought me, no matter how hard I tried.

I didn't have a name for why I was the way I was, but I could see symptoms of something. My most insidious symptoms – the ones most people never caught a glimpse of – were my shame, my sensitivity, and my wounded self-esteem. These beliefs that I was a bit useless and a lot lazy, had been galvanised over the years and started to close in on me from above, like bars. Not being able to explain my emotional intensity and rage was eroding my relationships. The niggling feeling that I was always failing made me defensive and over-sensitive. The cruel, berating self-talk that no one except me heard was getting louder and louder, as the lack of explanation for my inefficiency left me with no other conclusions.

By the time I was in my mid-thirties, I was chronically disorganised in a way that stressed out my whole family. I couldn't cope with all the moving parts, and what looked so normal for everyone else was requiring massive internal effort for me.

I tried to hide how hard things seemed for me. I promised my patient, concerned husband, Tom, that I would do better, and I would put down my head to get disciplined, efficient, and focused. Not following through on promises became embarrassing and I would hide behind my own frustrations with bluster and brashness, tossing out excuses and blame because I didn't have any other words to explain myself.

Most people couldn't see the cage I was living in, because I was still bright and chirpy and breathing. I could sing, but not soar. Those flip sides of the parenting coin had made me feel less like a paradox and more like a fake.

I had the most wonderful support from my family of origin and the one I married into. Tom was, and is, an engaged and empathetic husband, hands-on in ways that make me the envy of many. I had every reason to be okay, and yet, I wasn't. Of course, all this added to my confusion and shame for struggling so much. But, as it turns out, (I would later discover the research that confirmed this) motherhood was fertile ground for those dangerous, deeply-rooted beliefs to grow upward and over me. I was in over my head, and the cage was closing in.

During those early years of parenting, I also went on to get my Master of Arts in Vocational Studies (Cum Laude), preached at churches and spoke at conferences. Despite the outward progress, I found myself burnt out, with postnatal depression and on antidepressants. My marriage was struggling, and trust eroded between my husband and I as I battled to forgive myself for failing to follow through on declarations to do better.

I resigned myself to the labels of lazy, hazy and crazy.

Jess, you're just lazy. You can't finish what you start. You always procrastinate. It's so pathetic how you get overwhelmed and so you just end up doing nothing. What's wrong with you? Get your life together.

Jess, I know you thought you were smart but your brain is more than a bit hazy. I know how you get the details wrong when remembering a conversation, and it looks like you're hiding something or worse, making it up. It's not normal that you get so confused with schedules and feel so unorganised and stressed and stupid for getting easy stuff wrong. Everyone else seems on top of things. Why is this so hard for you, Jess?

You know what the worst thing about you is, Jess? You're crazy. You're too sensitive and too intense, saying things without thinking. It's so pitiful how personally you take things. Seriously, Jess, as Taylor Swift says: you need to calm down. You get so obsessed with something that you interrupt, or talk over people, or overshare way too much about yourself. I know how you overthink everything, and it's not normal.

At best, the cage made me believe I was a small person with a small life. On a good day, I could explain all of this with the resignation that I'm just not a high capacity person. At worst, the absence of an explanation made me feel irreparable. Without language for the problem, there is no hope for a solution. I believed I was hurting more than helping and my husband and kids would be better off without me, and the guilt led me down tracks no one should travel.

But then, I found the real "why." Suddenly, a key was dropped into that cage.

Many years ago, I came across this poem by the 14th Century Sufi poet and spiritual teacher, Hafez, also known as Hafiz. Hafez originally wrote it with a masculine character, but when I read it someone had taken poetic licence and changed it to a woman. I heard my story in a poem composed by a Persian man almost 800 years ago.

### *DROPPING KEYS*

*The small woman*
*Builds cages for everyone*
*She*
*Knows.*
*While the sage,*
*Who has to duck her head*
*When the moon is low,*
*Keeps dropping keys all night long*
*For the*
*Beautiful*
*Rowdy*
*Prisoners.*
*~ Hafez*

I had to write this book because I once believed a story that was not true. That story had to be retold. I knew what it was like to be a beautiful, rowdy, prisoner. Somewhere along the way, I had built a cage for myself and I didn't know who had the key.

Turns out, it was myself.

# DEAR BEAUTIFUL ROWDY PRISONER,

What kind of cage do you find yourself in right now?

Looking back, how has the way you've seen yourself changed?

What are some of the ways you describe yourself to explain yourself?

# CHAPTER TWO
## FREE AS A BIRD

*Jessica van Straaten*

*5 June 1995 (age 11)*

*Myself*

*My name is Jessica-Anne van Straaten. I like my name, But I hate it when people call me "Jessie." I'm rather tall for my age, which has its disadvantages, but most of the time I don't really mind. I've got a rather quick temper, and I'm very intense. Most of the time I'm happy, but I do have my ups and downs. I like to make people laugh, but not by fooling around. I've got a strong will, and I like to have my own way. Fortunately, I've got wonderful friends, and if they do get irritated when I boss them around, they don't let it show. I'm not a very soft person, and if someone is crying for a silly reason, I'm more likely to tell them to "shut up!" then ask if they're alright. But if I can see that they're really crying for good reason, I guess I'm rather kind. I'm rather good with little children, and sometimes do the babies Sunday school lesson. I love being around my friends, and I don't really like doing things on my own.*

*I love sport. I think I'm pretty good at swimming and I really enjoy it. I'm good at high jump because I'm so tall. I'm not very good at running. I'm terrible when it comes to a bat and ball, because of my poor eyesight. I have to wear glasses. Yuk. I hate my glasses and I can't wait to get contact lenses in a few years. I love cricket, even though I can't play, I enjoy watching it. I'm not mad about watching soccer on TV but I like playing it, even though I am not very good. But my best sport is swimming. When it's swimming season, I practically live for it. My Dad is a pastor, which isn't the greatest job, I think. I don't really like going to church, cause I don't have friends there. There are only two other girls my age, and they're both my sister's friends. I would much rather go to Rhema Lighthouse, because all my friends go there. But because my Dad's a pastor, I can't. I grew up in Empangeni, which is a really boring little town. I suppose it's better now, but when I lived there, the only exciting thing was when the circus came to town!!*

*No malls, no beach, no movie house, nothing! Anyway, I love Durban and I wouldn't move anywhere else, if I had the choice.*

*I think I'm sort of pretty. I've got brown hair, just past my shoulder, and I'm trying to grow it down to my back. I've also got brown eyes but I wish I had blue eyes. I've got very long legs. I'm thin for my age, which is a pain cause I can't wear bought stuff, it just doesn't fit. But I'm glad I'm not fat. I'm good with my hands, and I'm pretty good at art. I want to be an architect or an interior designer. I don't want to design hospitals or clinics, I'd much rather design houses. I forgot to say that I have an ugly nose. My mom and dad have got such nice noses but mine is all stubby and round. I hope it straightens out. I think I'm pretty clever. I'm ahead in most of my work, and I enjoy school (Most of the time, anyway!) I've got quite a good memory. I think I'm pretty good at drama. I got a 1st at Convention for expressive reading and a 2nd for poetry recitation. The play I was in also got a 1st.*

*Well, that's all I can think of for now. In brief, I'm a happy person and enjoy life. The only thing I want is contact lenses. Otherwise, I'm just glad I'm myself.*

*THE END.*

*Jessica van Straaten.*
*Std 4*

***

How adorable is this little Jess? I've left every little mannerism and error in the essay just as it was when I wrote it almost three decades ago.

When I read this essay to my dad he put his face into his hands and laughed. Shaking his head, he chuckled, "I'm going to read that out loud at your 40th birthday. Not much has changed!"

He's right.

That essay is a deeply accurate description of me today. Strong-willed, quick-tempered and constantly trying to hide my intolerance for people who cry for stupid reasons. I've joked that I don't "have" feelings, I am my feelings, so the "very intense" label is also still accurate.

When I read these words, I see such a confident little girl. She knows how to describe her unique Self, and not only that but she likes her Self. She knows what she's good at (swimming, art and having long legs) and she knows what she's not good at (running, ball sports and having a nice nose). She shows up as she truly is. She seems so fearless, honest and comfortable in her own skin.

I like her.

I see a little girl who enjoys doing things even when she's not good at them, and who knows she's not perfect but is happy anyway. She's proud of who she is, carelessly embracing what she isn't. She is fond of herself.

I love that little girl, because I remember what it felt like to be her – as free as a bird, uncaged and untethered. She was ready to launch into life and not only discover all the adventures out there, but boldly share her own beauty and creativity with the world. I know she had plans to soar to great heights.

I see her at eleven years old, laughing with her friends at a play rehearsal, pushing her glasses back up her stubby little nose.

But I also see her twenty years later.

She's sitting next to her mom, in the carriage of an old steam engine train with her family. They're heading to a Christmas market with Santa making his jolly way down the aisles for photos. Behind her gritted teeth, she's trying to smile at her in-laws and parents as they celebrate this festive family outing. She's barely holding back the tears, with two year old William on her lap. She's avoiding eye contact with her husband of eight years who is holding little six month old Luke.

Somehow, somewhere, she had lost herself.

It happened while she was looking out that train window chugging along the cliffside of a steep, rocky valley. She wondered what would happen if she jumped out – would she die straight away or would she just get badly hurt?

It sounds dramatic, but she was thinking that maybe if she was gone her family could be free of her. Tom could find a wife who wasn't angry all the time, her boys might have a mother that could cope, her parents wouldn't have a daughter who was snapping at everyone or crying or sleeping. She wondered – not for the first time, and not for the last – if they wouldn't just be better off without her. She was so stuck in a cage of shame, it had closed in around her without her even knowing when or where it started. All she knew was that the bars around her head felt so fixed, and so suffocating. And everyone she loved was trapped, too. Trapped because they loved her back and she was such a mess. She didn't really care what happened to her but she wanted them to be free.

I remember that version of myself because she longed for what most of us long for.

We all just want to be free.

Thankfully, not long after this train ride, I began the long journey of recovering and becoming myself again.

But in order to recover our Selves, we have to go back in time. Back to that free as a bird version, to remember that version of Self before the lies locked us in.

# BEAUTIFUL ROWDY PRISONER

# DEAR BEAUTIFUL ROWDY PRISONER,

Think back to a season when you most felt like your true Self.

What were you like when you were comfortable in your own skin?

Remind yourself about that Self.

# CHAPTER THREE
## MASTER OF NONE

I was born in a small town called Empangeni in the 1980s, in a sugar cane farming area on the east coast of South Africa, and I lived there until I was 8 years old. As dear little Jess mentioned in her essay, there wasn't much going on by way of over-stimulation.

My childhood was predictably routine and emotionally stable. I had a stay-at-home mom and a present, engaged dad in a happy marriage. My sister, Shani, was two years younger than me, a willing subordinate and even-keeled playmate in all our imaginary games. My youngest sister, Nicky, was born when I was six years old, and was a pleasantly cute addition to our family.

But I was, well, intense.

At the time, conventional wisdom for misbehaviour was a spanking, and I received many. My parents never hit me in anger, and it was simply part of life. We were sent to the bathroom to wait for Mom to calm down, then she'd come in, explain gently to us that what we had done was wrong and then we'd get two smacks on the bum with the wooden spoon. We'd cry, hug Mom and say sorry, and scamper off to play again. Apparently, in my case, there were times when this occurred two or three times a day and I was known to silently let my sister Shani take the blame for some of my misdemeanours. Sorry, sis.

When I asked my mom what all these hidings were for, she seemed to think it was mostly defiance. I was strong-willed, stubborn and had a very quick temper. Usually, my anger showed up in sharp words and occasionally a quick punch.

I remember in Grade 2 getting sent to the office and getting "jacked" by the principal as we called it, for hitting a boy during a game on the playground (it really actually was my turn, Clint). Another time, my friend Brent and I were sitting on the floor drawing pictures on a big chalkboard that was standing against the wall. I still remember how stupid Brent's picture was. He said it was a rowing boat. I told him it looked like a banana. We argued back and forth until I promptly stood up, balled up my fist and klonked him on the head with it. Needless to say, I was sent to the bathroom and had the wooden spoon for that – but I remember thinking, fair enough – I deserved it.

A more unjust incident was when I had built a tent in the garden out of bedsheets and blankets, and we had visitors over who had a smaller boy called Ryan. Ryan was probably about four or five years old, and he told me he was going to pull my panties down. I immediately responded by hitting him and was outraged that I got into trouble and he didn't. Another spank on the bum and a very begrudging apology.

It was a big deal that I couldn't master my temper.

I was educated in an unconventional curriculum from Grade 1 to Grade 9. Back then it was known as Accelerated Christian Education (ACE), and the model was that children worked at their own pace. It was all reading and writing, with very little verbal teaching. This environment was very quiet. You worked on your own, using subject workbooks that you read and wrote your answers in. Today, I'm sure there are many more kids being schooled like this, in homeschooling and classrooms, but it was pretty different for the 90s in South Africa. The teachers were known as supervisors and assisted us when we needed help by coming to our desks, so there was no teaching from the front of the classroom. We also never got homework, so afternoons were free to play. They were small schools, only 100 kids from Grade 1 – 12. It was a very gracious, forgiving environment in which to learn.

It was a wonderfully distraction free education, in a quiet room by myself with few sensory inputs. I could also daydream unnoticed, and do absolutely nothing without making it very obvious. I thrived. I was academically strong. I had a great memory, I could memorize anything and, because of the style of education, I flew forward.

The only subject I really struggled with was math, because you can't memorise math. It just never made sense to me. I tried to make math more interesting to myself, and developed what I later found out was called synesthesia. I have, for as long as I can remember, personified numbers. With no apparent logic, I had randomly assigned gender and personality to each number (for example, Eight is a nice girl, but Seven is a mean girl), and I used to make up stories about the sums I was doing by the types of numbers that were in it. Needless to say, I didn't get very far in math but it never really worried anyone because by the time I left the ACE system at the end of Grade 9, I was almost an entire year ahead.

It was in Grade 10 that I left my weird, awesome, safe, quiet little school and entered a "normal" mainstream government high school with 800 other girls. I thought I had died and gone to heaven. There was SO much to do!

For the first time in my life, I was in a classroom with a teacher standing up front, and though I remember getting kicked out of class many times for talking, my academic foundation, well-cultivated confidence and natural ability meant I went on to do really well there. Looking back, I had developed really good muscles for self-discipline back at my little ACE school. Working at my own pace, setting goals and getting on with it myself was normal by then. Mainstream school was organised and predictable with a consistent routine. Your parents dropped you off, the bell rang, and the throngs of girls carried you through the corridors to the right class. I was buoyed along by the rigidity of school life.

My two greatest challenges though were still math, and anything that wasn't in the normal routine, like tests. Not knowing how my odd ACE education would translate into mainstream, I had been placed in the 'lower' academic classes but it wasn't long before I was moved up to the 'A' class. Except Math. I was actually dropped down to the 'C' class for Math, which was such a relief because there I found my people, who also hated it and were way more fun than the serious girls trying to get to be Dux.

I was the dumb girl in the smart class, and the clever girl amongst all my fun, naughty friends in the other class. The academic girls saw how ditzy and scatter-brained I was, and yet I never struggled to get the marks. I was the girl who would arrive and everyone would be sitting outside with the noses in their text books and files.

"What are you guys studying for?"
"Jess, seriously? We have a science test today."
Oh. Whoops.
And then I'd get 80%.

I absolutely loved high school. I tried out for every activity. I was a jack of all trades, master of none, which I actually really enjoyed. Hockey, swimming, musicals, waterpolo, fashion shows, leadership committees, fundraising, you name it and I wanted to do it. I was absolutely confident that if I tried it, I'd be really good at it. I'd been a big fish in a small pond for most of my life and had won every race and everything in life. I ended up with Academic honours, being House Captain and the Deputy Head Girl. (I should have been Head Girl, obviously and there were rumours of swapped envelopes but I can neither confirm nor deny this.)

When I left high school, I fully believed I was going to take over the world. I had no idea what I was going to do with my life, except that it was going to be amazing and I would be brilliant at it. I was full of hopes and dreams, ready to soar. I did not anticipate that leaving the nest would end up with a failure to launch.

# DEAR BEAUTIFUL ROWDY PRISONER,

What hopes and dreams did the little kid version of yourself have?

What did your school experience tell you about yourself?

What labels did you leave your teenage years with?

# CHAPTER FOUR
## YOU NEED TO CALM DOWN

The deafening bass was pulsating through the black-walled nightclub, people milling around the balcony with its tacky silver railings. The crowd bounced and bopped on the dancefloor with hazy air that smelt like smoke machines, cigarettes and stale beer. I was with my girls at Night Fever, along with the rest of the Thursday night university crowd.

As the sound of my favourite song, Madonna's "Like A Prayer", came blaring over the buzzy speakers, I ran screaming onto the sticky dance floor and went totally wild. Suddenly, my friend Matt turned to me disdainfully, and looked down at me and said, "Geeeeeeez, Jess. You need to calm down."

I stopped dead. I can even now physically feel the visceral shame that flooded me in that moment.

I was too much.

Too extra.

Too hectic.

Of course, at the time I didn't link his snarky comment to the fact that I had previously rejected Matt's romantic overtures and told him his shirt was stupid. (It said, "Trust me, I'm a doctor" on it, and he was studying ***accountancy***. Idiot.)

University life came as a shock to me, and partying with my friends had become my outlet. The confidence and energy with which I threw myself into high school life had nowhere else to go. It felt like a force of energy that went from being a piercing laser to a lone, flimsy, flickering lightbulb dangling from the ceiling of an empty warehouse.

I didn't know what to study. So I decided on something broad and general, and chose a Bachelor of Social Science. It's a bit of humanities and it's a bit of business, and I'll figure it out, I told myself. It was too general, too boring and to be honest, too easy for me. I soon lost interest.

After one term of this disappointing foray into academics, I changed to a Bachelor of Commerce. I thought it would be more challenging and stimulating. Remember high school math? Now I was doing economics, accounting and quantitative management. You can imagine how well that went.

To this day, I still have a recurring nightmare about university. I am walking around campus and I know I have an exam somewhere. But I don't know what subject it is, and I don't know what time the exam is, and I know I haven't done the course work because I've been bunking lectures for weeks. It is the most stressful dream, because I'm waiting to be found out. Everyone is about to discover how useless, unorganised and irresponsible I am.

From an academic perspective, university was an absolute write off. I didn't even get marks good enough to pursue an Honours degree, and I really didn't care. I never had files for my notes, instead the back seat of my car was just covered in paper. Just before exams, I would find some really studious person (usually some hopeful, helpful boy who was eventually disappointed in my lack of reciprocity) who would have written all the notes out in different colour pens and photocopied them and made summaries and highlights. I would just take the notes and crash course memorise and absorb them – my very good memory and writing skills would save the day.

What ***had*** happened to me?

Somehow I had completely forgotten that as a little girl I wanted to be an interior designer, that I wrote poetry and did drama and loved the arts. I dragged my feet through the majority of my courses – commercial law, economics, management. I felt so stupid in the classes and didn't fit in with the type of classmates I had.

The first bar of the cage was coming down: maybe I wasn't actually that smart.

Maybe I was not an academically talented person.

Maybe I wasn't even ambitious and hungry for more.

Maybe I was just a bit of an average nobody with a ditzy, don't-care attitude.

All of these doubts and frustrations were drowned out with distraction – the beach, the boys, the nightclubs.

Then, at the beginning of my second year, I saw a poster in one of the campus corridors. It was announcing an international exchange program, and I spontaneously decided to go.

Within a few months, I was working at a summer camp in Canada, followed by one of the best seasons of my life at a university in Ontario. Now this was how I had imagined university life to be! I was cool. I was fun. I was interesting. No one wanted me to calm down. I could talk anyone into putting down their books and heading out for a night on the town. I made new friends and was always up for some random new adventure, from wakeboarding at lakeside cottages to snowboarding at ski resorts.

To top it off, all the modules I did on exchange were transferred back to my South African university simply as a "pass". Without an actual grade, it really wasn't evident how little academic work I had actually done. Could life get any better?

There was so much good that came out of these careless, carefree days. I came back to South Africa a changed person. I had always been indifferent to my business degree and had known it wasn't truly reflective of who I was. Canada was where I found another lens for the world – one that resonated with my values and beliefs. All my friends there were studying politics and international development, they were teachers and social workers and activists. I dated the editor of the school newspaper who was passionate and brilliant. He had convictions about the environment, women's rights, immigration and corporate responsibility – all new ideas for me. Bryn was so super smart and very good-looking that I didn't even mind how ugly his fair trade shoes were. We broke up because he liked to smoke a lot of weed, take shrooms and that was too much for me, but it was there that I learned about social justice. I had an awakening around what was right and wrong in the world.

I also joined a thriving, cool, student church that met on Monday nights in the on-campus nightclub and there I found an authentic faith that wasn't inherited, but owned. My spiritual growth was being stimulated and challenged alongside my own social awakening, and they became intrinsically entwined.

My intellectual brain also woke up when it was confronted with values and meaning. When I returned to South Africa for the final year of my marketing degree, I was done. I was not spending the rest of my life trying to convince people to buy things they don't need. I went from a mild indifference to marketing, to despising everything my business degree stood for. It was no longer out of insecurity, but out of principle. I just realised I wanted my life to count for something. I wanted to make meaning, not money. I mentally checked out of university and just went through the motions. I honestly don't know how I got through it.

Halfway through this final year of my degree, I met my husband Tom. Tom was gorgeous, brilliant and wildly adventurous. We spent the first six months of our relationship going camping, scuba-diving, mountain-climbing and exploring. He was much smarter than me, which I admittedly loved, and we would talk into the night about books and ideas, about people and purpose.

Two weeks into our relationship he said "I love you."

I told him I loved him too.

Three months into our relationship, he told me he wants to be a pastor one day.

I told him I already knew and I did too.

Six months into our relationship, he asked me to marry him.

I said, "Are you being serious?"

And then I said yes!

With my boring degree behind me, a brilliantly exciting and interesting man at my side, and a world of travel and backpacking ahead of me, I picked myself up and launched into the next season of life.

Life was diverse and interesting and never dull.

Tom and I spent two years working in London,where I did everything and anything – babysitting, working admin in a big corporate office, being a camp counsellor at a performing arts summer camp, being a receptionist at a fancy museum, working long hours in a start-up business with a bunch of wild, entrepreneurial women.

We backpacked through South America, worked an entire ski season in Aspen, Colorado and drove an RV across America stopping at national parks to camp and hike. I took Tom back to Canada and we worked at that same summer camp, making lifelong friends and memories in the place that had changed my life so much. Life was good. I was enthusiastically up for anything, and it wasn't too much to feel so much, dance so much, sing so loud.

Tom and I headed back to South Africa after three years of travelling, excited to start working at the church my parents had launched and pursuing our passion to love God, love people and make a difference. It was also time to start a family. It took me a while to get around the thought of putting the vocational career I had grown to love so much aside for pregnancy and parenting, but I thought I was ready.

There was no personal reflection on what was happening under the surface during my twenties. I had no idea that deeply rooted around me were some very dangerous beliefs about myself that – given the right conditions – could expand upwards and inwards, and if I ever found myself in over my head, might just lock into place.

# DEAR BEAUTIFUL ROWDY PRISONER,

Can you think of experiences in your past that made you feel foolish, insignificant or incompetent? What happened? What limiting self-beliefs were formed in those situations?

How would you complete these sentences about yourself today?

I am too ______________________.

I am not ______________________ enough.

What positive attributes would you like to be able to say about yourself?

# CHAPTER FIVE
## THE COVER OF THE PUZZLE BOX

"Will has ADHD, you guys."

I was meeting three of my closest friends for dinner that night and as I arrived at the table, late as usual, I sat down and burst into tears.

At the beginning of his Grade 2 year, we saw the light dim in our oldest boy's eyes. He would get into the car after school and burst into tears, having held back his frustration all day long. After some hits and misses, trying to figure out what was bothering him, we ended up taking him to an educational psychologist who came back to us with the conclusion that he was a brilliantly intelligent child, who also had Attention Deficit Hyperactivity Disorder (ADHD).

Over a large gin and tonic, my dear friends listened compassionately as I processed this "label". I knew nothing about ADHD. You could have told me my child had cancer. I felt like my hopes and dreams for this beautiful, dynamic, creative little boy had been built on sand and were crumbling away.

What did this mean?

What should we do next?

We had already been through so much trying to parent him the way he needed, and this felt like the final blow. The label, the diagnosis, the stigma – it felt like something had died. I sobbed and questioned and shared my fears, grateful for these wise women who didn't silverline this sudden reality. We had language for it, but didn't understand it.

Suddenly, I glanced across the restaurant and saw someone I knew sitting nearby – one of the bravest women I know. Her son, in his late teens, had an extremely rare disease and no one knew how to cure it. Their entire parenting life had been filled with specialists and trips around the country and experimental treatments, not to mention her son's physical pain and incredible suffering. She happened to catch my eye and gave me a warm greeting.

I sucked in a deep gulp of air and sat up straight.

My life was not over.

Our boy was going to be okay.

We would figure this out.

And, we did.

Over the next few years I took a deep dive into understanding everything I could about ADHD. I started with YouTube videos and progressed to interviews with international specialists who were the authority on ADHD. I followed Instagram accounts that were funny, read blog posts that were helpful and deciphered academic journals that covered the latest research.

The more I understood, the less terrifying ADHD was and the more things made sense. In fact, the more I understood, the more my own story started to make sense. It was like pieces of a puzzle that had always been there, laid out on the table. I had just never seen the cover of the box.

The final catalyst came along when I read some research about undiagnosed ADHD in women causing anxiety and depression. It was time to stop guessing and get to the bottom of my suspicion that for all these years of antidepressants and therapy, I had been treating a symptom not the cause.

Initially, I went to see a local doctor and I shared with her all the pieces of the puzzle I had been turning over. But, as I explained the process I had been on, I soon saw in her eyes she was trying to look like she understood – but she didn't. I basically diagnosed myself with ADHD in front of her, and she wrote me a script for Concerta.

That week, I was a mess on those meds. I cried three times at work and felt so intensely emotional (more than normal). So I did what any self–respecting adult who is making major life changes and needs professional input does. I put out a call on Facebook for adult ADHD specialists. I had barely clicked "post" when my phone buzzed with a name and number for a doctor. It was from a casual friend. I've since learned that this woman has a phone contact database I would pay money for. Her masseuse recommendation changed my life.

I digress.

I sat with the doctor's phone number for the morning, but before calling the office I voicenoted this friend and asked if she would share her story with me. I had picked up along the way that one of the keys to finding freedom was to reach out and ask questions.

I sat on my bed listening to her voice notes on repeat. There were light bulb moments in my head, going off as bright as the smile on my face. There were tears pouring down my face as I heard someone else put into words everything I'd been through myself. The realisation that I was not alone and that there was help for me, was like watching a lifeline appear in front of me. She dropped so many amazing words of wisdom in her messages to me that encouraged me to take the next step with my diagnosis. But the one that landed like a rock in a pond, rippling all the way to the edges of who I am was this phrase:

**Heal the mother, heal the child.**

Everything my boy needed from me was already in me.

But I needed to heal, and to scaffold and support my own capacity to give it to him.

I made the appointment.

Friday.

11am.

The day came, and I was so ready for it. Three weeks before the appointment, my new doctor had sent me dozens of forms to fill out, including one for Tom to complete. I already appreciated the thorough and professional approach, compared to my first experience.

The boys were on school holidays so I made a plan to drop them at Granny's house that morning. We arrived, and while they dashed off to play Minecraft like the well-balanced children that they are, I sat down at my mom-in-law's kitchen table to fill out the forms.

My husband's mom, Lynn, is an amazing woman. As I completed them, we chatted and reflected and laughed. She took a look at the forms, and gazed affectionately at me.

"Jess, I'm not a doctor but..."

We both laughed. It was so obvious.

I saw the time, grabbed my keys and headed for the door excitedly.

Two minutes up the road, I saw Lynn phoning me.

"Jess, you left all the forms on the table."

Of course I did.

I screeched back down the driveway, both of us giggling at the irony of this moment, and off I went to the doctor's rooms.

"Hi, my name is Jess Basson, I'm here to see Dr. M."

"Oh yes. Sorry, Jess, your appointment was an hour ago and we can't fit you in now."

Wait, what?

"It's 11am. Is it not for 11am?"

"No, your appointment was for 10am."

"But why did I think it was 11am?"

Embarrassment and irritation flooding my body, I reached for my phone to check my calendar.

The appointment was there.

For 12.30pm.

WHICH IS NEITHER THE TIME I ARRIVED, NOR THE TIME OF THE APPOINTMENT.

***What is wrong with me?*** Literally, the only thing I got right about this was the actual day.

"Unfortunately there's no space now, but Dr M can see you at 4pm this afternoon."

"Uh, yes. Thank you. That's amazing, thank you. I'm so sorry about this, that would be great, thank you so much, see you later, thanks."

Once in the car, I felt my whole body tense up and the self-flagellating story in my head began again. What started out as a quirky funny moment of leaving forms behind on a kitchen table ended up with an awkward and embarrassing arrival at the doctors. Holding back tears of frustration, I made a phone call to my long-suffering mother-in-law to ask if she could in fact look after the kids again later that afternoon.

The drive home sucked. I felt stupid. I hated inconveniencing my family. I was disappointed and embarrassed, and I realised how a million moments like this had slowly eroded my sense of competency.

Like a puppy caught pooping on the carpet, I skulked back to Lynn's house with my tail between my legs. Bad girl, Jess, bad girl.

By the end of that day, however, the cage door was unlocked with these clear, decisive words from Dr M.

"Jess, you are a classic case of adult ADHD, Inattentive type."

He paused dramatically, leaned over his desk and said,

"Now, listen to me. This is not the end of the world. You are going to be okay."

I burst out laughing.

"Dr M, I am not worried. This is the most liberating, wonderful thing I've ever heard."

This smart, funny, quirky doctor went on to translate much of what I knew about ADHD into adult terms. ADHD symptoms in a 6 year old little boy look very different to a 36 year old woman.

He gave me information about the average woman he diagnosed with ADHD. She:

Was about 32 years old.

Had been through a couple of rounds of depression.

Went through a major decline after the second child was born.

Had very likely been successful at school because most school systems reward inattentive girls with ADHD.

Had very likely struggled after school without the external disciplines, expectations and direction of school.

Would be better off in a corporate environment where the external schedules, meetings and rigid routines helped her stay on track.

Was likely to find that the worst job for her would be to be a stay-at-home mom, because she would have to be the origin and source of all the organisation, efficiency and smooth-operating of not only hers, but everyone in the family's schedules.

At one point, he mentioned the devastating role undiagnosed ADHD had on marriages, often resulting in divorce.

I could not believe it, but I also could.

It made sense from my own experience.

It made sense when I went looking for the research.

It made sense looking past symptoms and into the causes, the neurology, the physiological difference between an ADHD brain and a neurotypical brain.

Depending on one's age, gender, life circumstances, family environment, personality, intelligence and education, ADHD would show up differently for people.

Finding solutions is so much easier when you know how to describe the actual problem. While mine was ADHD, many people don't have the language for their cages – whether it's a diagnosis, or an addiction, or a habitual repetitive pattern in our lives that keeps tripping us up. There is no shame in finding a professional who will help you name the cage. In fact, the shame will grow stronger without the truth. Maybe the professional is a psychologist, or a pilates instructor, or a nutritionist. Maybe it's a debt counsellor, or a spiritual home, or an addictions recovery programme.

The key is to reach out and ask for help.

Now.

Because once you've seen the cover of the box, the puzzle pieces are easier to find and fit together.

I believe that understanding your cage is not only liberating, but can save your relationship, career, self-esteem and even your actual life. Whether it's ADHD or another mental health challenge, when the underlying causes are actually identified, they can be treated correctly. We can find the appropriate support and practices to truly, freely live. To have the quality of life we may have given up on.

I knew I wanted that for myself.

Not just to survive.

Not just to sing from inside a cage.

But to actually soar again, to be fond of myself again, to live without shame and walk into the light knowing who I truly am. I wanted to lift the lid off my head, and be in wonder and awe of the vibrant, flourishing, creative brain that lived inside of me.

There was an element of sadness and regret with the realisation that I had become a small woman, building cages not only for my own brain but for everyone around me. I wanted to be a sage, I wanted to use wisdom to drop keys for others.

Like a detective, I went back to those early mothering years where the wheels had officially come off for me, looking at the puzzle pieces with new eyes. The ones between having babies in 2011 and finding this diagnosis of my own in 2021. There had been a whole decade of the cages closing in, and now I had a key.

Back when my boys were toddlers, I had begun writing. I blogged and wrote articles in a local magazine as The Rookie Mom. Moments of mothering madness became moments of hilarity. In the online world of perfect Pinterest families and shiny, happy mommy bloggers, I found a little corner of the internet that loved my messy version of all this. As I shared the honesty, the connection and the vulnerability with which I was processing life, I discovered there were a lot of us struggling along. People loved knowing they weren't alone. On the other end of the spectrum, I suspect some readers felt good about themselves knowing there was someone out there (***Hi! It's me!***) who was a proper hot mess. People loved knowing they weren't that bad after all. My funny little blog was a comfort to both ends of the spectrum.

As I reread those old blog posts, I found my undiagnosed

ADHD written all over them, just waiting to be picked up and turned into answers for some very important questions. Turns out, when you have the picture on the puzzle box to help, there is a very satisfying clicking into place.

For fourteen years, I had been practicing content creation and communication. Through all of the struggles in my head and home, my work had been somewhere where I still felt competent and proud of myself. Opportunities came up for me to not only preach, teach and lead in my church job, but to facilitate and coach in the business world, and dive into dialogues and projects with non-profit organisations in the social justice space. I consulted with schools and did speeches at functions. Wearing so many hats was one of the strengths of my kind of neurodivergent brain, and adapting to different contexts was not only interesting but I had become adept and skillful at it.

In my mid-twenties, I took a look at all of the different hats that I wore to find the common denominator and from this, crafted my personal mission statement. I wanted to spend my life "communicating life-transforming ideas".

From church stages to corporate workshops, from magazine articles to blog posts, I had spent thousands of hours teaching others about the intersection of helpful, established, challenging truths with their own story. Very often, I did this by sharing my own journey, sharing what I had learnt the hard way.

As I share this journey, I invite you to not only spectate mine but search for yours. May you find the cover of your box, so you too can stop puzzling and start soaring free. You can absolutely find freedom, one step at a time moving out of the darkness and closer to the light you were created to live in.

# DEAR BEAUTIFUL ROWDY PRISONER,

When last did you reach out and ask for help?

What are you currently puzzling about that you need help with?

Who is someone you could reach out to?

# CHAPTER SIX
## ADHD AND ME

DISCLAIMER:

*Please note that I am not a medical professional nor a mental health professional.*

*The content in this chapter is intended to provide general information about the symptoms of ADHD in adults and is not for diagnostic purposes. The objective of this chapter is to create awareness and understanding.*

*Should you recognise these symptoms in yourself or in others, please be motivated to take the next step towards health and support. ADHD is often diagnosed in conjunction with other factors, and symptoms can have other causes.*

*Nothing here replaces talking with your healthcare professional to assess your condition and determine the need for a treatment plan appropriate for you.*

***

ANOTHER DISCLAIMER:

*Whether you have ADHD or not, you might become aware that you need support for your own mental health. You may resonate with my emotions and experiences, but for completely different reasons. What matters is moving towards a healthier self regardless of the cause of your struggles. Please seek out mental health care and practices that help you to do well.*

***

PROBABLY THE MOST IMPORTANT DISCLAIMER:

*This is a little heads up. You might not agree with me. That's okay. We're both still okay. If you feel yourself getting your knickers in a knot, go make some tea and give yourself permission not to feel personally attacked by my views and opinions expressed here. If it helps, you can even roll your eyes and snigger and sleep well tonight knowing you are superior to me.*

*Actually, that might give us something in common because I am not losing sleep over it either.*

*Either way, there are three beautiful opportunities for you here.*

*You can:*

*Grow in your awareness and learn something new.*

*Choose compassion and empathy for those who have ADHD, whether or not you agree with their diagnosis or treatment choices.*

*Or pat yourself on the back for being more knowledgeable than me.*

*Whichever way it lands, good for you.*

***

Accurate explanations lead to active problem solving.

If you don't know what's going on in your brain, body, or soul, it's going to be much harder to find freedom from the cages that have closed in on you. Hopefully, this book will prompt you to ask the questions at the end of each chapter so that you can find out what cage you're in and how to get free.

This chapter is an invitation to sit like a fly on the wall of my life, and watch me do a puzzle with the box cover in one hand, and hundreds of pieces spread out on the table. You're going to have to figure out what your own puzzle box cover looks like. You'll have to identify all of your own pieces on the table. But hopefully after watching me do it, it will feel a little less scary and maybe even be rewarding.

Puzzling along with me is the main reason for this chapter, but I confess this: ***I do have another agenda.***

I really want you to understand ADHD. Why?

Because there is a very good chance that someone you know has it.

Someone you love and care about may be stuck in the ADHD cage.

Maybe it's your mom, or your partner, or your kid.

Or your best friend's child, or that friend of your son, or the child you teach.

Maybe it's your colleague, or your business partner.

Maybe it's you.

If you picked up this book because you want to grow into an uncaged version of yourself, then this chapter might be like when you go to pay for a gorgeous new shirt at the check-out counter and then the cashier tells you that you're getting a free handbag with it. Bonus! You came here for some help and humour, but you're getting even more than you bargained for.

Because you know the kid I'm about to write about. And this kid needs you. They need you to see them, and understand them.

Whether the kid is your own little one, or their friend, or that girl that's giving them a hard time at school, this is what life is like for ADHD kids.

Listen. They are trying so hard. They want to impress us, please us and be liked – they want it so, so much. Sometimes, they're trying so hard to be okay that we don't even know they're hurting. Sometimes, it's been so hard for them to mess up again and again, that they've given up trying and now it looks like they don't care.

I know their meltdowns, and their tempers, and their behaviour can be scary. Trust me, when they lose it, it's terrifying for them too because they can't make it stop. After the outburst, the flood of shame is soul-killing because they actually do know better. They know better because you taught them what is good, and they can't do it, and they don't know what's wrong with them. Hopefully, you'll not only catch a glimpse of how incredibly empowering an accurate explanation is, but you'll learn enough to liberate someone special in your own life from the myths and misunderstandings surrounding ADHD.

***

## WHAT IS ADHD?

When I used to think of Attention Deficit Hyperactivity Disorder, I would picture a little boy who is bouncing off the walls, fidgeting in class, interrupting the teacher and being destructively distracted. I discovered there is much more to ADHD than the common stereotype, and thankfully more is being researched and revealed about this condition each day.

Before we move on, though…

We've all seen ADHD used to justify lazy, negligent parenting and a lack of discipline. Perhaps like me, you've seen overmedicated kids and labels tossed around way too easily. I remember years ago, a friend who is a doctor told me that she could tell which teacher from which school couldn't manage her students' behaviour because of how many kids from just one classroom were referred to her for "ADHD" and "Ritalin". It was statistically impossible that so many children from one class could have ADHD. Those kids didn't have an ADHD problem, that teacher had a behaviour management problem.

On the other hand, more diagnoses are emerging as more people discover they have ADHD, because we have simply become more accurate at understanding and recognising this disorder. This means more people can get the appropriate help and support.

Some adults today should never have been diagnosed with ADHD – they remember the lights going out of their eyes on the meds. Other adults wish they had known this about themselves when they were younger. They see now how it would have helped them avoid so much heartache and struggle.

Sadly, the lack of understanding as well as the casual, careless over-diagnoses have added to the shame and stigma for those who actually do have ADHD.

The bottom line is that when we know better, we can do better. When we know better, there will be less random throwing around of the ADHD label as an excuse, and more reliable diagnoses for those who truly need the intervention and support.

To understand ADHD, a helpful phrase that is working its way into everyday language is the term "neurodiverse". In the late 1990s, the sociologist, Judy Singer, who is on the autism spectrum herself, came up with a word to describe conditions like ADHD, Autism, and Dyslexia. This word was "neurodiversity". Her hope was to shift the focus of conversations away from the usual words of deficits, disorders, and impairments. She helped to emphasise the idea that different people think differently – not just because of differences in culture or life experience, but because their brains are "wired" to work differently.

Neurodiversity is a scientific concept arising from brain imaging. A number of brain studies have shown that people with learning or thinking differences really are biologically working differently than their peers. Without going into all the detail, studies using MRI scans show that when compared to a neurotypical brain, the neurodiverse ADHD brain shows actual physical differences in white matter and shape. These differences are consistent with remarkable accuracy. Brain imaging shows how, while performing the same task, neurodiverse brains will use different parts of the brain. In other words, some children are born with brains that think, learn and process information differently than others. Remember, it is estimated only about 4% of human brains have ADHD. If we lifted the lid on these beautiful brains, they would look different from the average, neurotypical brain that the rest of the population has.

ADHD is a neurological divergence, not a behavioural disorder.

***

## TYPES OF ADHD

Every person with ADHD looks different.

I have my own biology and personal history, my own personality and context, my own temperament and stage of life – all of this flavours my brand of ADHD. They say if you've seen one person with ADHD, you've seen one person with ADHD. The reason there are so many ADHD symptoms is because there are at least three different types of ADHD. Some professionals get more detailed, suggesting up to seven types. The technical terms have changed over time, but broadly speaking you have:

The Hyperactive-Impulsive Type (this is the well-known one).

The Inattentive Type (formerly called ADD).

The Combined Type (a combination of both Hyperactive-Impulsive and Inattentive).

Most of the symptoms listed in the Diagnostic and Statistical Manual of Mental Disorders (DSM) are obvious and external – we see them in people's behaviour. What is harder to identify are the less visible symptoms, like emotional regulation, thinking patterns and sleep difficulties.

For example, I have always needed a lot of sleep. I now understand that having a nap every day after school and university (which is what I did!) was how my brain regulated itself after an overstimulating day. Sleep helped me slow down my ADHD brain and recover, so when sleep disappeared (hello babies!) the wheels came off.

This is why both research and personal story-telling are so important – it helps us to see ourselves in other people's experiences, not just in technical research.

If you'd like to take a deeper dive into the different types of ADHD, there is a useful summary at the end of the book that shows the symptoms of the three main types with some reflections from me on how I've experienced them.

For now, let me lift the lid on my neurodiverse brain and how ADHD shows up in my world.

## THREE THINGS I'VE LEARNT ABOUT ADHD AND ME.

### BRAIN LIKE A FERRARI, BRAKES LIKE A BICYCLE.

One of the most famous explanations of ADHD was by Dr Russell Barkely, who said:

"ADHD is having a brain with the engine of a Ferrari and the brakes of a bicycle."

My brain can go from zero to one hundred in a few seconds, whether it is coming up with an idea in a brainstorming session, or having a lightbulb moment in a conversation with a friend. Our ADHD brains are fast and often connect dots that others haven't made yet, which is why I'm strategic, creative, and love finding patterns and connections in life. The power of the ADHD brain is the ability to focus for hours on things that are fulfilling, taking deep dives into conversations or topics, and really enjoying small details that neurotypical brains overlook.

This is because ADHD is not a deficit of attention – we have plenty of attention. It is a dysregulation of attention. Because while our engine was designed by Italian engineers, our brakes were borrowed from a kiddies bike at the store. Slowing down, taking a corner, changing directions, and even stopping ourselves in our tracks is really difficult. An ADHD brain has a hard time shifting its attention from one thing to another in the same way that a neurotypical brain does.

When a doctor asked my seven year old if he struggled to finish his work at school, my son described himself like this.

"It's like I'm thinking about one thought, and then another thought comes along, and then I don't know which one to look at."

Let me say it again: ADHD is not a deficit of attention, it's a dysregulation of attention. This struggle to regulate applies not only to thinking, but also to emotions. Ever heard Katy Perry's catchy pop song, ***Hot N Cold***?

"You're hot then you're cold
You're yes then you're no
You're in then you're out
You're up then you're down."

I used to think this song was about a toddler.
Now I know it's about someone with ADHD.

From my own "quick temper" in my childhood, to my struggle not to cry at work when someone confronted me, my bicycle brakes affected my emotions and still do. Emotions are intense and moods can swing, and this is hard on our relationships. ADHD brains can have strong adamant opinions, and overreact to things, erupting like a volcano – and then be fine a few minutes later. Sometimes I experience this dysregulation as an emotional distraction – a conversation is too boring, a task is too stressful, an article is too confusing. The emotion is so strong that it overrides the self–control to push through or refrain from interrupting.

Why the word "deficit" at all? It's not attention, but

neurotransmitters that have a deficit. Studies show that the ADHD brain does not produce, distribute or consume key neurotransmitters in the same way that a neurotypical brain does. Think of these neurotransmitters as WiFi signals – they carry the information around. If the WiFi signal is weak, your downloads take a long time. Your text doesn't send. The video keeps buffering. The page stops loading halfway down.

The great actor and comedian Will Ferrell once said, "Before you marry a person you should first make them use a computer with slow Internet to see who they really are."

Slow Internet? Welcome to the ADHD brain.

Sometimes, the message is delayed and arrives late. ***(Is that the time? Flip, I'm going to be late again!)***

Sometimes, the messages all come crashing in at once like when you've been out of signal and suddenly your phone starts going off and every text and email and notification arrives at once.

***(I cannot stand this dinner party one more minute – too many people, my shoes hurt my feet and I hate the song playing in the background. *walks outside mid-conversation)***

Brains like a Ferrari.
Brakes like a bicycle.

## TIME BLINDNESS

If I asked you to book a weekend away at a cottage in the mountains on 2 November three years from now, you would probably look at me like I'm a bit bonkers. My husband Tom might be able to handle it because he is a productivity genius with a life plan and goals, but most people would feel like that's too far ahead to commit to something.

This is because the time horizon for the typical brain is about three months. You can't really place yourself in time beyond that.

You can't tangibly see yourself that far into the future, or relate realistically to what you might be doing.

What's the average time horizon for an ADHD brain? Two to fourteen days. Not only do most ADHD brains live in the now, but we also don't experience the passage of time the same way that neurotypical brains do. Time feels different to us. Some call it time blindness.

My husband Tom is an amazing athlete who has run every distance from ultra marathons to obstacle course sprints. He will tell you that your pace depends on how far away the finish line is. You have to know how much distance you will cover in order to decide how much effort to put in.

If you understand time, you can pace yourself.

If you don't understand time, you can't.

Often, ADHD people seem unmotivated because they'll sit around doing nothing until the last minute. But our brains only respond to the urgency of the now because later is such an abstract concept. Why do something now that you can do later? Only later isn't actually later, and suddenly the deadline is here and I'm pulling an all-nighter.

"I thought I had more time! What happened to the week?", said every ADHD brain ever on a Friday morning.

Large, long tasks get very overwhelming for ADHD brains and we need lots of mini-deadlines looming over us all the time. We are sprinters, not long distance runners.

Time blindness is why I don't give myself enough time to get ready for things, or assume I'll get more done before I have to go. Time blindness is why I arrived one hour early for my very first job interview and just sat outside the building in the snow waiting for my appointment. Even before I knew I had ADHD, I didn't understand time properly and I didn't trust myself to get it right. Time blindness is why my darling, dearest friend with ADHD told us that on our girls weekend away we were going to wake up, have some quiet prayer time, make a quick brekkie, do an online pilates class and finish with a slow walk through the forest – all before we left to go home at 9am. Our clever non-ADHD friend worked out that we would have to wake up at 3am if we were going to do all that.

Time blindness.

The struggle is real.

I know that It's hard to imagine someone struggling so much with something you take for granted. On the other hand, the struggle for me was that only I knew how much effort it took for me to do something everyone else seemed to manage quite effortlessly. Sure, I masked it and came across as normal most of the time – but it took an enormous amount of energy and often made me anxious.

Another way our time blindness and dysregulation of attention shows up in the ADHD brain is in our hyperfocus. Hyperfocus is like when one message is being transmitted and that is all we can pay attention to. It can be incredibly effective at times if you know how to harness it. It can also be why ADHD people forget to eat or reply to messages or run errands. When we are in the zone, it's hard to get our brains out.

In a child, hyperfocus might look like being so engrossed in a TV show that they do not hear anyone calling them to turn it down, or asking them to come to dinner. Of course, for the parent this seems like wilful disobedience and defiance. Discovering this neurological challenge for the ADHD brain was a lightbulb moment for me as a parent. So often I had called my son over and over and over again, getting louder and louder and eventually shouting at him – only to see him look up at me in surprise, as if he was hearing me for the very first time. Turns out, he had no idea why I was standing there losing my mind at him for ignoring me because he had just heard me for the first time.

For an adult, hyperfocus might be picking up a book to read for a few minutes before bed and then finding yourself bleary-eyed and still reading into the wee hours of the morning, even though you know you're going to be exhausted the next day. I just can't stop.

One of the ways hyperfocus shows up in conversation with ADHD adults is that they get stuck on a topic they're passionate about. I know that I can interrupt, dominate the conversation, bring it back to what I was saying even when everyone else has moved on and then I die a slow death as I realise how awkward I have just made it for everyone. Hyperfocus sounds like someone telling anyone who will listen how great the new Taylor Swift album is without realising no one is as into it as they are.

Sorry everyone I met in 2020.

You can see how time blindness comes across as socially inappropriate. Often ADHD people feel insecure, embarrassed or misunderstood after realising in retrospect how awkward they may have been. I feel like I need to go have a nap after just writing this section.

***(Jess excuses herself to curl into a fetal position and eat a brownie)***

I'm back! What was I saying again? I've lost my train of thought…oh yes.

## WORKING MEMORY

Finally, one of the most helpful ADHD traits I've learnt about is how effectively my brain uses working memory. Which is to say, it doesn't.

We have three ways to store memory – working memory, short term memory and long term memory. Working memory is how you process the information you're receiving right now and how you respond to it in the moment. My ADHD brain is like a whiteboard that runs out of space, and so I have to erase information I'm still using in order to take in the new input.

This shows up as forgetfulness...what was I just saying? This shows up as losing things...where did I put my phone?

This shows up as absent–mindedness…why did I walk into this room?

This shows up as extremely annoying for everyone... especially yourself.

One of the reasons I have always hated cooking is because I get so flustered. I never knew why until I realised that following recipes was frustrating because I could never remember what I had just read!

Me baking:
**4 cups of self-raising flour**
Goes to get flour out of the cupboard, walks to the drawer for measuring tools.
Was it one cup or half a cup?
Goes back to the recipe book.
**4 cups of self-raising flour.**
Fetches one measuring cup.
Opens the flour bag, scoops in two cups of flour.
How many cups was it?
Goes back to the recipe.
**4 cups of self-raising flour.**
Oh, it's four.
Scoops in one more cup.
How many did I already put in?
Dammit.
Wait.

It's supposed to be ***self-raising*** flour?

But for the meals I have totally memorised, it's easy. They're in my short-term memory which is great. My long term memory is even more incredible. This is how I got five A grades in high school (***all the memorising subjects***) and one D grade (***math – the processing current information subject***).

It's not totally hopeless for ADHD brains. We just need systems that bypass working memory and rely on our short-term memory. For example, I will walk into the house, put my keys down, go get some water and then have no idea where the keys are. But if I always hang my keys on the hook, I don't even have to use my working memory. I rely on short term memory to find things. That's why routines, habits and schedules are so key for ADHD brains. This poorly developed working memory can make ADHD people seem irresponsible, careless, and like they are ignoring instructions. You're seeing it now, aren't you? In floods the negative feedback, criticism, berating self-talk and poor self-esteem.

How liberating to realise ADHD is not a behavioural disorder, or a character issue like I believed I had – it's a neurological divergence.

It is critical for ADHD to be explained, because just like a person with diabetes can't try harder to bring their insulin levels down, I cannot rely on sheer willpower and determination to make my brain work more effectively. In fact, only having the "Try Harder" tool is what decimated my mental health in the first place. Instead, I had to take ownership. Acknowledging that someone has ADHD is giving them the opportunity to choose ownership instead of making excuses.

What happens when someone is diagnosed with ADHD? There are fewer excuses and more explanations.

One of my ADHD mantras is, "No, you won't."

I simply had to become more realistic with myself. When I would get a message on my phone from the school saying there's a parent evening coming up, I used to tell myself, "Oh, I'll put it in my calendar later when I'm sitting at my laptop."

No, you won't. Do it now.

When I drop my keys onto the couch instead of hanging them on the key rack, I used to tell myself, "Oh, I'll put them away when I tidy up this evening."

No, you won't. Do it now.

I can explain to myself that my brain will ***not*** remember to hang up the keys later and then all hell will break loose when the whole family is looking for the car keys in the morning and we're late and I can't remember why they're not on the hook where they are supposed to be.

Once I was diagnosed, it helped my marriage, because we had better explanations for my behaviour. My long-suffering, gracious husband Tom is more understanding with me now. Understanding has given him so much more empathy, which helps both of us not freak out or become resentful. It has helped him not take my absent-mindedness personally and he has been so gracious to adapt and adjust to more realistic expectations.

The most liberating gift ADHD has given me is that since I've been diagnosed, I'm changing the story about myself in my head. I am trying not to explain myself using every negative, self-hating adjective in the book. I am unlearning all the sad, cruel, self-pitying explanations for why I was the way I was, and deciding not to shame myself.

I'm daring to dream again, try again and start to imagine what I can do with my time and talents again. I'm giving myself permission to rediscover that eleven year old girl. I am now more realistic about what she needs to actually achieve her goals, and I'm taking ownership of putting the right support in place.

I actually ***can*** finish what I start – if I have routines and external accountability.

I actually ***can*** push through losing interest – if I break the task down into having urgent "now" deadlines, and give myself rewards for getting started on a boring job.

I actually ***can*** stop being the screaming mom – if I learn to know my triggers, prepare for them, and take my medicine.

An ADHD diagnosis is not an excuse. It's an explanation.

Realising you have ADHD is not an excuse to procrastinate, overreact, forget important details or get overwhelmed. It's an explanation that helps you be more realistic about what might happen to you under certain circumstances and how you can set yourself up to do well.

***

But Jess, these "ADHD" symptoms. Everyone does some of those things. Yes, they do. You could probably tick off a whole bunch yourself. The important question is why.

If someone has a headache, she could be dehydrated, or tired, or have forgotten her meds again.

It could also be because she decided to go buy a big, cool headband like the young people wear because it's trendy and that was a bad call so stop trying too hard to stay young, Jess.

Symptoms are one thing.

The "why" is the game changer.

Maybe you resonate with some of these symptoms but you're also sleep-deprived because of a baby, or incredibly stressed out because of work, or have just experienced a major life transition, or you have other health complications.

Self-diagnosis is a launch pad as it often gives you permission to take the next step. Professional diagnoses are key, especially when there are other mental health issues to factor in, like depression or anxiety.

Like most neurological disorders, ADHD exists on a spectrum. For some people, their ADHD is so severe it is extremely debilitating, and for others it is mild enough to manage quite easily and without too many interventions. My ADHD is often masked, and then triggered by my environment and the demands of different seasons of life. A specific ADHD diagnosis can be found by assessing the cluster of the above symptoms, plus the impact it's having on the quality of someone's life. I often get told not to label my ADHD, or not to call it a "disorder". But leaving ADHD unnamed means leaving it untreated. As my story shows, this can have a negative effect on many aspects of life, including work, relationships, and mental health. If there isn't an accurate explanation for the cluster of symptoms such as trouble managing time, impatience, disorganisation, forgetfulness, and mood swings – the effects can be devastating.

Accurate explanations lead to active problem solving.

Puzzling out the cover of your box is so important and may involve a combination of personal reflection, rigorous research, listening to others stories, and seeking out professional help. In the same way, solutions to the problem will be multi-faceted. There were many lightbulb moments that helped me to name my cage, and there is no silver bullet for a comprehensive solution.

What are you going to do to bring more understanding to the cage you find yourself in?

## DEAR BEAUTIFUL ROWDY PRISONER,

Could there be a puzzle in your life that you haven't seen the cover of yet?

If you have a sense of something you need to learn more about, what are your next steps?

What did you learn about ADHD that has changed your perception of this diagnosis?

How might you support or advocate for people with ADHD in your life?

*IF YOU THINK YOU OR SOMEONE YOU KNOW MIGHT BE LIVING WITH UNDIAGNOSED ADHD, PLEASE REACH OUT TO A MENTAL HEALTH PROFESSIONAL, PSYCHIATRIST OR DOCTOR WITH A SPECIAL INTEREST IN ADHD.*

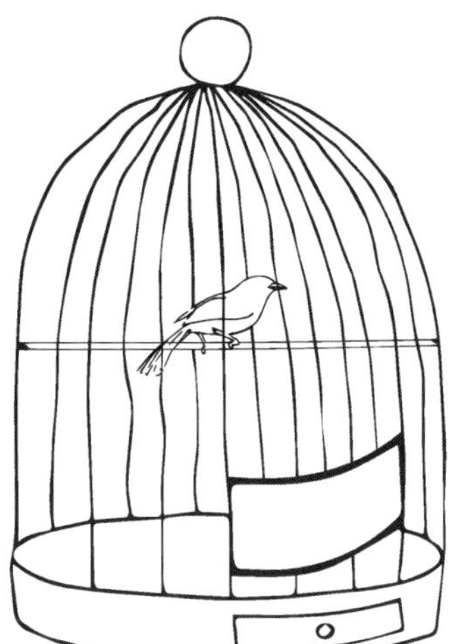

# PART II
## DROPPING KEYS

# CHAPTER SEVEN
## HOW TO CURE A MOMBIE

You may be wondering what a Mombie is, but you've seen her at the Mall. I know how to recognise them because, for about two years, I used to see one in the mirror everyday.

Dark rings under her bloodshot eyes.

No make up.

Cereal smeared down her shirt.

Stumbling a little, and possibly talking to herself.

Her toddler is crying because he can't hold his truck ***and*** his juice bottle in the same hand. The baby is licking the handle of the trolley. Inside that trolley you've seen the standard Mombie shopping list – wine, rice cakes, and cartoon-themed yoghurt. Because we all know that yoghurt with Spidey on the lid gives you superpowers.

Mombies survive on coffee that's been microwaved four times because there's no such thing as a coffee break in this office.

Mombies can pretend that the shark is eating a whole spoonful of pirates – in other words, get a two year old to eat chicken-a-la-king. She may or may not be feeding a teething baby homemade pureed pears at the same time.

Mombies don't wear a messy bun because it's cool, she wears it because having a shower is more of an every-few-days type of luxury.

Mombies also wonder if they're the only ones out there who have to do this stuff. They wonder if they're the only ones who feel like the walking dead. Every Mombie wonders if she's the only one who feels this alone, who finds it so hard.

Is it really meant to be this hard?

When I was a Mombie, I felt a little indignant about this whole motherhood thing.

It's difficult. Like, really difficult.

But there are so many women out there doing this all the time!

Apparently there are 2 billion mothers alive right now. This is not a rare, dreaded condition. It made me think, "It can't be that bad. It can't be so hard. Why would so many people be doing this if it were so hard? It must be just me." Based on how many mothers there are out there, my conclusion was "I'm the only one who is struggling this much." Thinking you're alone is a recipe for chronic Mombie symptoms. You start to feel you're losing your mind because this seems to be so effortless for everyone else.

One of the worst things a Mombie can do is to hide the truth.

Why do we do it? Why do we post statuses about our fantastic weekend, and Instagram our perfect children with their matching clothes and personalised hashtags when actually we cried in the shower that same morning? Why do we chat enthusiastically about birthday parties and the sale at Woolies and whether or not 5G is the cause of the coronavirus (***insert conspiracy theories here***) when secretly our brains are melting in our heads from sadness? Then, when the other mom in the playground asks us how we are, we smile and say fine.

Even when WE ARE NOT FINE. Even when we are so sleep deprived we think we might be depressed, and when our marriage is a mess. Even when deep down we are so afraid that we will never be good enough.

No wonder it feels like we're not really living, like we're waiting to feel alive again. We long to be present instead of distant, we long to be real instead of fake. Hiding is how you make mombies – the living dead, going through the motions. Dragging our feet, lurching from one moment to the next. Being a mombie is dangerous for everyone nearby.

As it turns out, I had started hiding my mess long before

motherhood made me a mombie. Because I learnt that the messy version of me could not be discovered.

When I was about ten years old, we went on a school trip and my teacher was so horrified by the state of my cupboard after just a few days, she took a photo with her film camera and printed it to show my mom how messy I was. I was so embarrassed, and angry with her. I couldn't believe she took a photo of the inside of my cupboard and went to all the effort of printing it at an actual photo printing shop. Self-righteous old bat. I might still have some rage about that moment. I might still not like her now, when I bump into her at my mother-in-law's golf club.

In high school, you could rarely see the floor of my bedroom. Have you ever seen a teenage girl get ready to go somewhere? Try it on, take it off, throw it on the floor. Repeat several times.

At university, it was my car. Files? Who puts their notes in files when the back seat of your car works just as well?

I was a mess.

Step into my life at the young age of twenty-one – my very own Thomas Owen Basson. This is the man whose DVDs were alphabetised (back when people owned DVDs). This is the man who has his calendar colour coded and his life goals categorised. This is the man who I know is not in a good place when he starts rearranging the books on ***my*** bedside table to relieve his stress. When Tom got into my car the other day, he told me it gives him the hives.

When we first got married and were living in a little flat in London, we had to figure out how to live in the same space with such different approaches. Tom wisely realised that he couldn't stop Jess the Mess. Off he went to the shops and came home with three washing baskets. One for darks, one for lights, and one for anything lying on the floor that belonged to me.

I'm not unorganised, I'm just untidy.

Actually, I am a little unorganised but it's not as bad as it looks.

The truth is, whether you're ten or twenty or almost forty, life soon teaches us that being a mess is unacceptable. Being a mess is uncomfortable and awkward. It is not okay to be a mess.

So we start to hide our mess.

Not in washing bins and cupboards and cars, but behind our gritted teeth and clenched jaws. We hide our mess because we are ashamed, and afraid that if anyone sees behind the door, they will be disgusted and walk away. We're afraid they will try to fix us, change us. Most of all, we are afraid that if we show anyone the mess, no one will love us.

Hiding is one of the primary causes of Mombiehood.

So what is the cure?

The antidote to hiding is honesty.

What every Mombie needs to start coming back to life again, is a shot to the heart of honesty. You can call it authenticity, or vulnerability, or truth-telling but it is like putting on an oxygen mask for someone who can't breathe. Honesty can resurrect you.

Choose honesty instead of hiding.

When the boys were babies and toddlerish, I had the kind of twenty–four hours that come along every now and then, and turn moms into zombies overnight. Everyone except me had the flu. I was up four or five times that night, had about three collective hours of sleep, and two incredibly cranky kids in the morning. I posted a "joking-but-not-really" Facebook status about having a Mommy Meltdown, and soon after I received a text from a good friend, Christie.

"Are you okay? Can I come over with ice cream and rocky road?"

(Sidenote: every Mombie needs a friend whose love language is food).

My first reaction was to lie. To hide behind the socially acceptable answers.

"No, don't worry, I'll be fine, we'll be fine." I started typing this out as I hid in the bathroom. I was in my pyjamas and the house was a wreck. My two year old was screaming on the Naughty Chair, and who wants visitors at 8am when you just want to ugly cry? Besides, it just seemed so weak. So useless. Which it was a little, but I was also so desperate. Before I could overthink it I deleted the original and banged out, "Yes. Please come. I need some help." Send.

Christie arrived about twenty minutes later, and I kid you not, she had a cooler box on wheels with home-made ice cream in it. I didn't even know those existed. It was like a classy ice cream truck except the flavours were fancy grown up ones like white chocolate and toasted coconut ice cream.

Of course, it was a little awkward for me to let someone into the mess, into the frustration. But, it was so worth it. I was sick of faking it, sick of pretending that I'm okay when I'm not, and sick of feeling alone. I didn't have to be. There were other options – so why choose it? Looking back, I wonder why I waited to be such a mess before deciding to be honest. Honesty was delicious.

We sat on the kitchen floor and ate ice cream and I vented-slash-laugh-cried. It felt so liberating to just be real and let someone into what was really going on. Honesty cured me a little that day because it brought me back to life. Brené Brown says that the only way to be engaged and alive in our lives is to be vulnerable. I don't want to be a zombie who just goes through the motions – I want to feel alive, and if that requires being honest and vulnerable, then so be it. If honesty cures Mombies, then take a deep breath and be brave. Brave enough to tell the truth and ask for help.

If you're a Mombie, stop faking that you're fine and ask for help. Tell someone what's really going on behind the scenes, and be brave enough to let them in. If you know a Mombie, help her to be brave and give her a safe place to take the mask off when she comes out of the everything-is-fine closet.

Take her some ice cream, too.

# KEY 1:
## CHOOSE HONESTY INSTEAD OF HIDING.

What have you been hiding from others?

Who could you tell the truth to?

Imagine yourself showing someone one of your behind-the-scenes.

Notice what you feel as you picture that scenario playing out.

# CHAPTER EIGHT
## LARGE FOOT, BIG MOUTH

I have big feet.

Like, size 8 big feet. That is a size 41 in the EU. That is a size 8.5 in the USA. That is a size BIG in whatever country you're from.

I seldom paint my toenails bright colours because there is just so much surface area. On a normal foot, coral pink toenails look sweet and summery. On me, it looks like I spilled a tin of paint on my feet. I call my feet roadmaps. Because of all the veins.

This, however, is not my primary problem. My more worrying dilemma is not where to find shoes that fit, but how often I put my large foot in my even larger mouth. I'll say something I'm not supposed to, or blurt out what everyone else is thinking but has the good sense to keep quiet. I've spent many a dinner party getting my knee squeezed under the table by my husband, who is basically begging me to stop talking. I just keep going on in a way that is actually pretty impressive. I'll bring up paying your domestic worker a living wage, or talk about how women get paid 28% less than men for doing the same job. At one point, my particular activism obsession was focused on fair trade, sweatshops and consumerism which is how I made a pleasant evening rather awkward after I found out I was sitting opposite a buyer for a large, cheap, fashion chain store. I mean, I just wanted to know if she'd actually been in the factories in China where they get the clothes, but I see now that it was a little weird for everyone. Classic Foot in Mouth Disease symptoms.

As you can imagine, these conversations are about as fun as the shopping mall the week before Christmas.

Knowing what to say and when to say it is quite the art, I

am still learning.

Because sometimes you just need to shut up.

But also, you know what else?

Sometimes you don't.

Last weekend, I went to a baby shower. I know. You already feel sorry for me, but this one wasn't that bad. There were no eat-melted-chocolates-out-of-nappies games, and the glowing mama-to-be didn't have to guess what was inside every gift. We didn't even have to write down what we thought the circumference of her belly was to win a prize, which I appreciated.

You could tell it was a special baby-shower because I even made choc chip cookies.

With an oven.

And ingredients.

From scratch.

Using a recipe.

Just when you think you've got me figured out..I bake!

Anyway, I was chatting to one of the few women there who did not have children. This isn't by choice, and she has had some heart-breaking miscarriages. Despite the risk of putting one of my Big Feet into my notoriously Big Mouth, I decided to go with my gut instinct and I asked her, "How are these things for you?"

She told me that she only went to baby showers of people she really loved. She told me how she didn't want to be excluded from something important in their lives. She told me these mornings were hard mornings.

But then, she turned to me with big eyes, and said, "You know, Jess, you are the first person who has ever asked me how I feel at baby showers. Thank you!"

I was quite surprised that it meant so much to her, and asked her to tell me more. So she did. She told me how, when she had a miscarriage, there were people who deliberately avoided her. When they saw her coming, they walked the other way. When she lost a baby, there were people who knew about it but never, ever mentioned the experience to her.

Sometimes, you really don't need to be quiet.

A few days later, I had almost the exact conversation with a teacher at my son's school. This beautiful family had lost their teenage son just a few weeks before. He died an unexpected, tragic death. She shared with me how her daughter's closest friends had just shut her out. They didn't phone, they didn't message, and this young girl was hurting so much more than necessary. As I looked at the hurt and disappointment in this mother's eyes, I remembered the same look from my friend at the baby shower. It hit me.

Say Something.

When someone you know has lost a loved one, or is dealing with an exceptionally overwhelming situation, say Something. Please don't pretend like you don't know. Please don't ignore the most real thing that is happening to them.

Just say Something. Even if it's, "I'm so sorry for your loss. I don't know what else to say." They've already lost something. They don't need to lose a friendship or a connection that brings joy and love into their lives. They've already had an experience that makes them feel different from you, now you're adding distance in your relationship? Grief is a lonely experience, and if you don't know what it feels like, don't pretend like you do. But for goodness sake, don't ignore them. They need you more than ever before.

Not long after coming out of the hiding-your-mess closet and choosing honesty instead, I realised that I had not practiced the muscles of showing up for people because I had held them at arm's length. I had not really witnessed what it meant to show up for someone until Christie and I had our early morning ice cream on the kitchen floor confessional.

You can't give what you don't have.

Which is how I ended up almost missing opportunities to say Something.

One evening I was sitting with my mom, and telling her about how overwhelming my week had felt. A special friend of mine who lived overseas had just spent two days in hospital with her three year old who had undiagnosed cardiac and respiratory problems. Then, I got an email from another close friend who found a lump, and was letting me know because the results weren't back yet. Just a few days later, another friend had to rush her husband to hospital at 3am after he inexplicably collapsed. As if that wasn't enough for one week, I sat with a friend whose marriage was on the brink of collapsing. They had two small kids.

I felt a little overwhelmed by all the pain people were going through, and I didn't know what to do or say.

"You're probably used this by now, Mom." I said, sighing. "These hard, horrible things that just seem to happen all at once, to such good people."

She didn't answer right away. But when she did, it was gold.

"Jess, to be honest, I've learnt to accept it. I've learned that it is inevitable. That pain and hardship is inevitable. I've just come to peace with the fact that we are each going to suffer in some way. But if you can get through it, if you can manage to get through it, you realise that it's because of this suffering that we grow. It's because of this pain that we mature."

She carried on knitting.

"When it's over, you will never forget the people who cried with you. You remember the text messages, and emails, and you know that you are loved. Sometimes all you need to know when you're going through terrible pain is that someone is thinking of you."

Silence.

My mom just busts out profound stuff like this while we're watching Schitt's Creek.

"But Mom, you kind of have to believe that suffering makes us grow. Otherwise what other conclusion can you come to other than the world is just a shit place?"

"Jess, for me it's true because I've experienced it. It's not just something nice I tell myself to get through hard times. I believe it because that's how it happened for me."

Then she told me the story of an old family friend who was on holiday by herself in the United States, where she had a terrible horse riding accident. Her husband was back home in South Africa but had gone camping in a wildlife nature reserve, and it took them three days to track him down to tell him what had happened to his wife. Our friend, who still can't walk properly to this day, told my mom how when she was lying in that hospital bed, alone on the other side of the world, wondering why this had happened to her, she'd get a message from someone miles away.

*"Thinking of you. Praying for you. Love you."*

She said that's what helped her to hold on.

Simply knowing that there were people thinking of her and praying for her.

Simply knowing she was not invisible.

I don't know what your faith is, what your thoughts on spirituality are, or what you believe about God. Maybe you pray, maybe you don't. I do know that no matter what you believe, people need to be seen and loved. When they can't fall pregnant, or they've lost someone they love, or they're getting divorced or they're just not coping with motherhood – they need to feel seen and loved.

SEND THAT TEXT MESSAGE.
PICK UP THE PHONE.
DROP OFF SOME FOOD.
SAY SOMETHING.

It doesn't have to be profound or life-changing or have all the answers. It really, really, really doesn't need to be advice. It just has to say "I love you", and maybe a few reasons why. Share your favourite memory you have of them, or of the person that they've lost. When you say Something, when you show up, when you recognise someones' reality with them, you make their hard things into ***our*** hard things.

I've heard that Foot in Mouth Disease is highly contagious. Perhaps, like me, you won't always get the timing right or have the exact words when you open your mouth to say Something. You may even miss the mark completely and get a kick from someone under the table. In most cases, Something is better than nothing.

Say Something.

# KEY 2:
## SAY SOMETHING

Is there someone you're avoiding?

What could you do to reconnect?

Think of someone who might feel invisible.
How can you make them feel seen?

# CHAPTER NINE
## I HAVEN'T ALWAYS BEEN THIS WAY

It was a mild KwaZulu Natal winter and our whole extended family went on an absolutely idyllic holiday down the South Coast. I'm talking about warm sunny weather, clambering over rock pools looking for crabs, building sand castles in the little bay into which a burst sewage pipe flowed giving everyone in our family chronic diarrhoea and vomiting for the entire ten days.

That's right.

Idyllic.

After four nights of changing bed sheets and syringing medicine into a baby's throat, I was done. The boys had woken up at 4.30 am and I had to get them out of the tiny beach cottage so everyone else could get some more sleep. I was pretty sure my younger sister would be arranging a vasectomy for her fiancé when they got back to Cape Town. At 6am, I packed the two kids into the car and drove to the local beachside mall called the Shelly Centre – I wasn't even sure it would be open. There the three of us walked around the mall for an hour, looking into the windows of the closed stores and waving at the staff who stared at us as they arrived to open the stories – me, Will and Luke in our pyjamas! My pyjamas were old grey cotton harem pants and a navy oversized hoodie from university days. Did I mention I was wearing my bright purple Nike running shoes that I use for gardening? It was a highlight in glamour for me, personally. But it was a low point in my mental health.

Later that day, I was standing in a kid's playground pushing one of the boys on a swing, and crying on the phone to a very dear friend, who also happened to be a very good doctor, about how much I was struggling. She very gently said, "Jess, I wonder if you aren't a bit depressed."

The thought hadn't occurred to me. Really? Depression?

When I was fourteen years old, my mom had experienced burn-out and depression, and for her it looked like sleeping and crying. I was more like raging and ragged nerves. The idea of having depression caught me off guard. I knew I wasn't okay and I had been trying so hard to pull it together. I was going to see a psychologist, and had close friends praying for me. This definitely helped but couldn't seem to break the cycle of anger and disappointment that oozed out of most interactions with me. Trying harder and failing was sucking me down into a spiral of more hopelessness.

When something creeps up on you, it's hard to recognise what it is and give it a name. Especially when it's sneaking in through the darkness of thoughts you are telling no one.

There was quite a lot I wasn't telling anyone.

Just a few months before this disastrous holiday, we had been on that Christmas train. I knew I was in trouble when I looked at my family and thought, "They'd be better off without me," but I still hadn't told anyone how dark my thoughts had become.

My dear friend Kath's gentle suggestion about depression was a lightbulb moment. I don't know how the truth broke through those dark clouds I was surrounded by – it was one of those sacred moments but suddenly I had a clear, distinct thought in my head.

"I haven't always been this way."

I used to be different. Somehow, through the clouds and fog, I remembered. I remembered what I used to be like. After my next emotional meltdown, I tearfully said to my family, "This is not normal. I haven't always been this way...***have I***?"

That night as I lay in bed, I looked up postnatal depression. I found an amazing website and when I started to read through symptoms, I just knew I had to take the next step.

I had ticked all the boxes of what you're ***supposed*** to do. Go for counselling, eat well, exercise, sleep more, get help from family and friends. Done, done, and done. But this wasn't enough. I discovered that there was more to depression than sadness and crying.

For me, depression was a roller coaster of rage.

On the good days, it was mild irritability that I could keep at bay if the day stayed relatively unstressful. I could laugh and socialise and get things done. I could play with my kids and make dinner. Most days, I didn't "look" depressed. One of my favourite writers, Glennon Doyle, says: "People who need help sometimes look a lot like people who don't need help."

On the worst days, I would feel myself holding back the tears. One little complication would flip me over into a ranting, raving person who just wanted to run away. I would apologise and apprehensively watch the people I love try to forgive me again and again, knowing how tired they were of these patterns. Either way, anxiety and nervous controlling energy were always simmering under the surface.

I had postnatal depression. Having words for this was the beginning of freedom. I could name it, so I could tame it.

## NAME IT TO TAME IT.

We can be afraid of labels or diagnoses, but we also can't get the right support without knowing what is wrong. Whether it's your emotions, the state of your marriage or the harsh reality of your financial situation – you gotta name it to tame it.

I woke up the next morning, after reading and researching, and I went to Tom, my sister and parents. I told them I am not okay. This is not normal. There is something wrong with me and I needed help. With a call to my psychologist and doctor, I started on antidepressants that week. There in that little beach cottage where we had spent the week being really really sick, I took a big step towards becoming really really healthy.

I remember standing with my dad in the lounge looking out at the beach, holding an antidepressant pill in my hand. I had never been on a daily medication before and it felt so official. I said to my dad with tears in my eyes, "It just feels like such a big commitment." He held me against his chest, looked down at me and said, "My girl, it is a big commitment. It's a commitment to healing and recovery."

Within two months of taking my antidepressant pills, I felt like someone had cut the rope that had been dragging me down, and the heavy weight sank to the bottom without me. I could breathe fresh air again, and feel the warmth of the sun on my face, and when I blink into the light and look around me, I feel like me. Like me, before the pregnancies, before the hospitals and the breastfeeding and the sleepless nights and the overwhelming anxiety.

When you've been lost in anxiety and depression for three years, you can forget who you really are. You can start to believe the lie that you are simply the worst kind of person. Because you try to be different, and then you try harder, and then it still doesn't work. So you end up resigning yourself to the lie that you are categorically a weak, awful human.

I had the most incredible support system – my husband, my parents and parents-in-law, my sisters. Ironically, many of my closest friends are either doctors or psychologists or life coaches! In that season, they were all so helpful, from the first tough pregnancy to adjusting to being a stay-at-home mom of two.

I went on to learn that this unusually supportive and healthy environment may have enabled me to get that far without actually realising I had postnatal depression. A combination of a strong support system with relatively mild depression can easily be missed. We had managed to keep it at bay. But depression is a chemical imbalance in the brain, and unfortunately no amount of loving support is going to set that right.

As I started to recover, this was what I told myself regularly:

"Depression is not who I am. Depression is something I have. I have it, it does not have me. Lots of people have depression and anxiety. But there is no one out there who has the unique personality, temperament, character and identity that I have. And those things have not changed. I am still me. Taking antidepressants has simply allowed the chemicals in my brain to balance back to how they were created to work, so that who I am can come shining out again."

I still get angry and stressed and anxious. Like my normal self used to. In fact, I have actually learnt how to deal with anger and stress better now, because all those during months of depression I was desperately trying to learn the necessary skills to cope. I went to therapy. Tom and I went to marriage counselling. I read books about parenting, marriage, and God. I prayed and I journaled. While these things were not enough to fix the serotonin levels in my brain, they are skills that I have now practiced. It seemed like they weren't working – but actually, I was learning how to communicate, how to identify what I was feeling and how to take care of myself.

Now those skills work.

Now they are super helpful. I'm a better person because of those skills.

But self-improvement and skills are not going to fix chemical imbalances.

I am healing. I am recovering.

I am trying to make amends with those I hurt and disappointed.

I am learning more about grace and kindness than I ever knew I could.

But I had to name it to tame it first.

# KEY 3:
## NAME IT TO TAME IT.

What do you need to find language for?
Perhaps you just don't know what exactly is happening, or maybe you do know and you just don't want to acknowledge it.

Is there something about yourself that you've forgotten along the way?

Who do you know could help you remember what you used to be like?

Decide on a step you can take to help you recover that part of yourself.

# CHAPTER TEN

## GET A DIARY, LOSKOP

We woke up on a Monday morning, and I could feel the post-holiday blues setting in. Gone were our six weeks of summer break, our lazy mornings of swimming twice before 7 am, the whole family hanging around on the verandah, and no school departure time looming. I knew I needed to prepare my four year old for the imminent disappointment of School Days and a new school year that was about to begin.

"William, today is Monday. That means it's two more sleeps until Wednesday when school starts again."

Oh. My. Word. The child's face. He looked at me blankly. As the news registered, the look of dismay devolved into despair. Silent tears started rolling down his cheeks and he threw himself onto my bed.

"I'M NOT READY! I'M NOT READY!"

Can you say heartbroken? Because that is how we both felt. I looked at his tear-stained face and how he tried to pull himself together. He's only four! Should the prospect of school be THIS devastating? He should be playing with glee and learning with delight and discovering the world around him enthusiastically. The thoughts whirled through my head in a few split seconds.

Change schools. Complicated.

Homeschool. Definitely not.

Move to a small-holding in the rural Midlands countryside where the children can roam wild and free while I grow kale and raise goats? I'll look up properties for sale.

I took a deep breath and talked him through it. He loves his school, and we worked out it was the prospect of a new teacher that was freaking him out. The moment passed and we all recovered, determined to make the most of our last few days of holidays.

About two hours later, I realised I had THE WRONG DAY.

School was only going back the NEXT week. There were nine sleeps until School Days, not two.

What the heck, Jessica? Get a diary, woman.

I resolved to be more organised in the new year that lay ahead. I bought an actual diary, a wall calendar with magnets, and a pen with four different colours. I gave myself a personality makeover.

You see, I usually leave the colour-coded organisational charts and spreadsheets to my husband, who is an efficiency and productivity guru. This is hardly my field of expertise, as I'm more of a big-picture, go-with-flow kinda girl. I'm the ying to his yang, the chaos to his categories, the sleep-in to his self-discipline. I bring balance to the Force. Just call me Yoda.

There is a great Afrikaans word: "loskop". Directly translated, it's los = loose, and kop = head. Loosehead. Instead of using the entire phrase "If your head wasn't attached you'd lose it", you can just succinctly say, "Oh my word Jess, you are SUCH a loskop."

In my defense, there is an upside to being a loskop. Being somewhat all over the place or "free-spirited" as I call it, is essentially my charitable act of service to the community. For example, I keep receipts, tissues and empty smoothie cups on the floor of my car for one main reason – to make you feel awesome about your less-messy-than-mine car. Can't find your sunglasses? That's nothing. I'm on my third pair in two months. (Admit it, you feel better about yourself now). If you're still not sure what I mean, I can send you the photos of my 18 month old son eating ice cream.

With brownies.

And M&Ms.

At 8.30 am.

For breakfast.

If you have kids, you should be fist pumping the air and claiming "Parent of the Year" for yourself because everything is relative.

I am a messy, unorganised, often a bit confused person who hasn't made a list of personal goals since 2005 and now you can feel awesome in comparison.

You're welcome.

But New Year's Resolutions, as we all know, can be futile and short–lived as my blank diary and lost calendar magnets proved. Was there a way to transform Jess The Mess into Jess the Best?

No, there was not. But I did realise if I wanted to change, I had to choose it. No silver bullets. Just small choices.

Good choices make great changes.

I knew I wanted things to be different, but wanting was not enough. If I wanted to make changes, I had to make some choices.

I pressed pause on giving myself a personality makeover fueled by mom guilt. I re–examined my ambitions with three filters to help me choose what to change.

### CHOOSE ONE THING TO CHANGE.

Trying to do an entire life overhaul is not realistic. Setting too many goals means you will inevitably fail to accomplish some. With every failure you will become more demoralised, and eventually, you will give up on them all. So choose one thing that you can actually achieve. The more realistic your goals, the more success and happiness you will feel as you accomplish them. Start small with one step.

### CHOOSE TO ADD, NOT SUBTRACT.

This means deciding to add something positive to your life, instead of just trying to stop doing a whole list of unhealthy things.

You could decide to end the late night cookie binges, quit smoking, stop watching so much Netflix, and go to bed on time. Or, instead, you could decide to just add one thing to your life, like start walking early in the morning three times a week. If you focus on adding something positive, many of your negative behaviours will naturally decrease and fall away. I asked a friend to walk with me, and knowing she was also waking up at 5.00 am, and that I would disappoint her if I bailed, helped me get up and do it.

## CHOOSE SOMETHING THAT MATTERS.

If you're just making a change because you "should", you will struggle to sustain the change. Rather choose something that you really believe in. Instead of saying, "I want to be fit", say "I want to be able to play sports with my kids". For me, I felt bad about stressing my kids out because I didn't know what day school went back. It affects our social life, my babysitting plans, how I manage my commitments, and time. Buying the diary helped me map out the first few months of the year, and it felt good because not stressing my kids out matters to me.

For so many years, I swung between feeling sorry for myself and feeling angry with myself, instead of choosing something good for myself. I would take the first and necessary step of recognising my emotions and acknowledging them, but then get stuck there and allow them to determine my next move.

I know it's not easy. But take ownership. Make one good, small, helpful choice at a time.

# KEY 4:
## GOOD CHOICES MAKE GREAT CHANGES.

What one thing would you like to change at this moment?

What is something positive you can add to your life that would affect this one thing?

Think of a value that is linked to this one thing.
How can you frame this one thing in a way that is meaningful to you and who you want to be?

# CHAPTER ELEVEN
## EXERCISING IS THE WORST

"Oh, that Jess. She is such a fitness fanatic. You should see her exercise, she's incredible!" said no one ever.

I hate exercise. I don't like being tired, I don't like being sweaty, and I don't like being useless at something. When I was a teenager, I was quite good at swimming. I trained daily with a swimming club that had a real coach, and a pool, and everything. I hated it. I would tell my mom when I woke up in the morning that my stomach was sore, in preparation for a major health complication I had planned for after school, so that my excuse to not go swimming at 5pm would seem more legit.

Admittedly, I've faked liking exercise. When I was dating my husband Tom, I went mountain-biking with him. On a mountain. We went surfing together quite a few times. I even used to train with him in his home-made gym, and let him shout and count how many pull–ups I did and time me on the skipping rope. The things you'll fake for true love.

I want to be a better person. I just don't know where to start. The problem is if I say I'm going to get fit, eat better, keep my cupboards tidy, manage my time more efficiently, have more quiet meditation times, and just be better at everything in the whole wide world – then I know I will get overwhelmed and eat a pack of ham while watching reruns of 30 Rock. I've done it before, and I'll do it again.

My list of excuses about exercise included, but were not limited to:

1. I don't need to lose weight.

2. I am one of those annoying people who is just slim. Without the pressure of vanity, exercise seems a complete waste of time.
3. I have a fast metabolism and my ridiculously noisy stomach is proof that my digestive system alone can keep me fairly slender (see point 1).
4. Exercise makes you sick. I am the only one who didn't get the flu this winter even though I didn't exercise. My husband Tom, who uses things like assault bikes and heart rate monitors and muscles, has been sick twice. Ha. Research ***that***, scientists.
5. Exercising is selfish because it's all about you and I'm a martyr who puts other people first.
6. I hate being sweaty.
7. I don't have time to exercise because I work, study, mom, wife and a bazillion other things that are simply more important (see point 5).
8. I really want to be more disciplined but <insert whiny voice here> "It's soooooo hard."

I just have this very strong gravitational pull towards laziness. It's like a vortex that sucks me in until I've given up and go back to scrolling through my phone on the couch instead of doing all the things I should be doing. I happen to be very good at being lazy. I hide it by walking fast and looking stressed so that people assume I must be accomplishing a lot but I'm actually just really, really lazy.

There was a time when I tried to be better. I decided to start swimming again, and as it turns out it was really good for me. Because it provided documented evidence that I am the worst at exercising.

I confess to you now, the deterioration of my discipline…

## DAY 1

First day of exercising. I've bought a new swimming cap, and a new costume, so I feel very slick and professional. I make babysitting plans for my baby boy, Will. I arrive at the gym, get changed and stand on the edge of the pool. The sun is shining in through the large, glass, windows. The pool is quiet, the water smooth and still.

BAM! I'm in.

Wow…I'm actually quite fit.

Like, really fit.

This feels so good. I can feel my back muscles waking up. My legs are a little useless (i.e I barely move with the kickboard) but apparently carrying around a 10kg child for half the day gives you some rather kick-ass arms. I'm not saying I definitely stopped to admire my biceps, but it's possible. I start lapping the old lady next to me, and I imagine breaking a record at our local fresh water long distance race, the Midmar Mile. I can see myself crossing the finishing line, walking out the dam and waving at my family with a big, not-breathless-or-dying smile on my face. Maybe I should set a more challenging goal than doing Midmar. I mean, children do it.

50 laps done.

***

## DAY 2

Based on my recent swimming accomplishments, this should be a cinch.

BAM! I'm in.

The plan is 10 warm up laps, 10 legs, 20 arms, 10 warm down.

My goggles keep steaming up so I'm taking a little longer to get into it today. Also, that nice feeling in my back muscles is gone, and they don't work anymore. With my stroke suffering, and my piddly little legs contributing nothing productive to the scenario, I'm not moving quite as fast as last time. But still, I clearly have to push through. This is what discipline is all about. Pushing through. Overcoming. I try to make up a compelling Tweet while I count my laps.

What?

A stitch?

I haven't had one of those since the inter-house gala back in '99. Need to drink some water.

Okay, obviously I'm having an off day. Who needs to warm down when you swim as slowly as I do?

40 laps done.

***

DAY 3

My kettle-belling husband has informed me that 30 minutes of exercise twice a week won't get me fit. I'm pretty sure that it's a scientific fact that if you have a stitch while exercising, you're getting fit. I decided to do half of the session with just the kickboard, because it will work my legs, which is a big muscle so you get extra fitness points. Also, I'll swim 50 laps again instead of 40 like last time.

OMG.

There are at least 3 band-aid plasters on the floor of the pool, which is kind of disgusting. And, that's just in my lane. I wonder if they're from the same person? Who swims with so many plasters on? How did they injure themselves? How many laps have I done?

Well, using the kickboard is obviously like swimming twice as far because it's twice as much energy, so according to my calculations I've sort of done about 36 laps, so I'm going to round that off to 50 and get in the sauna.

50 (36ish) laps done.

***

## DAY 4

It's raining. The gym air–conditioner is on freezing because of all those annoying fitness-obsessed-weight-lifting-fitness-obsessed people upstairs. I slide into the pool, and consider just getting out and going to the sauna again. I'm pretty sure it's a scientific fact that if you're sweating, you're getting fit. But I remember that my mom is babysitting my son so that I can get fit, not daydream in the sauna and get a Peanut Butter Bomb smoothie.

Grrrrr.

I swim, but to reward myself for being so disciplined, I finish early.

30 laps done.

***

## DAY 5

I go straight to the sauna and then get a Peanut Butter Bomb smoothie.

0 laps done

But who is even counting anymore?

***

Can you see the vortex? Did I even stand a chance? How can you possibly overcome steamed up goggles, and coldness, and sheer bloody-minded laziness? I knew this would happen. As usual, I tried to start again but this time with even less confidence in my ability to be awesome.

My pep talk to myself was pretty awesome, though.

"I'm starting again. I'm getting back on the wagon. Back in the pool. And back in the sauna. No, just the other backs. Not that one. Back on the pool wagon."

Confession: I got back in the sauna.
Exercising is the worst.

# KEY 5:
## NO EXCUSES.
## JUST EXERCISE.

I know. I wish I was wrong.
No matter what your cage is, exercise will help you unlock the door.
Go for a walk.
Follow a silly dance routine on YouTube.
Sign up for yoga.
Do it alone. Do it with someone.
Just do it.

What is your next step to do more exercise?

# CHAPTER TWELVE

## PURSUE PRESENCE, NOT PERFORMANCE.

I have two gorgeous tattoos, one on each of my forearms. I designed them myself and I love them to this day. People often ask me what my tattoos mean, and their first guess is usually the names of my children. While I was a mom when I had them needled into my skin, the words themselves were written on my heart long before I had kids.

I was twenty seven years old, and I was working as a youth pastor. I was building teams and running programmes for teenagers to explore their faith and grow spiritually. While I was cheered on and loved as a person, our church culture had a patriarchal background, and this showed up in well-meaning people's unconscious bias. Or sometimes not unconscious. Like when I regularly got asked if Tom was going to "help" me with the youth department I led, or when I was questioned about whether I was going to have children before the go–ahead was given to study my Masters. ***(Because why would you spend all that time and money studying if you end up staying home with the kids, right?)*** I was often the only woman in the room, and so I had to come to this job with everything to prove.

My whole identity was wrapped up in being a great leader, and I was running hard in pursuit of performance. I eventually hit a wall in terms of my health, and ended up really worn out and tired. That wall was a chilly, sunny winter morning on 14 June, 2010.

It was the middle of the school holidays, and everyone in South Africa was buzzing with the energy of hosting the FIFA Soccer World Cup. Along with youth programmes from all over Durban, our teens were part of the team running a soccer holiday club at an under-resourced, overcrowded urban school in the city centre. It was a big project with lots of moving parts.

The day the programme started, I woke up to discover that I had lost my voice. I wasn't sick. I didn't have the flu. I just lost my voice. I literally could not speak. When you are coordinating lifts with parents, directing volunteers, and helping out with more than one hundred little kids at a holiday club full of sports, activities and games – this makes you absolutely useless. And being useless was my ultimate nightmare. This was not a Disney's The Little Mermaid moment, where I silently went on to adorably hand signal my way to success with a singing crab to help me.

This was an identity crisis.

My worth and significance was coming from what I had accomplished, and when I couldn't perform anymore, it left me empty and confused. Suddenly, I was forced into silence on the sidelines. I went from being in charge to being a spectator. It unravelled me.

I remember sitting on the side of a netball court, watching my team explain a game to a group of kids, and being so frustrated that I couldn't get involved and tell them what they were supposed to be doing. I was trapped and furious about it. No one puts Baby in a corner! Except for mental health. That will put anyone in a corner.

Pursuing performance was going to push me off a cliff. Someone needed to grab me by the scruff of my neck and tell me to slow down.

I know I'm not alone in my pursuit of performance. Some of us are pursuing the ideal husband or wife or kids. Some of us may be aiming for the grades, the body, the interior décor or the lifestyle that we hope will make us feel good enough. Perhaps you're chasing the perfect career path, or crafting the perfect reputation. Those of us who run this hard at our goals know it is exhausting.

Not everyone is chasing perfection, though. Sometimes we're just trying to outrun our imperfections. Perhaps you have your head down and you're just trying to get as far away as you can from what happened. Maybe you're trying to just stay ahead of the expectations that nip at your heels every day when you wake up. Avoiding that mess with frantic busyness and productivity, trying to prove that you're more than something that was done to you, not by you.

No wonder we're so weary. Trying to outperform our imperfections is impossible.

Feeling like a voiceless Ariel trying to get Prince Eric's attention happened to me on one specific day, but recovering from it was a much longer process. As part of my physical, mental and spiritual recovery from burnout, one of my spiritual mentors from church sent me on a silent retreat. Clearly, being quiet was something I would have to be forced to do.

Off I went to spend 24 hours in silence at Coolock House, a Catholic retreat centre. I arrived at this place on the South Coast, alongside a beautiful coastline, and when I walked in I was greeted by one of the nuns.

"You look tired", she said kindly.

"I am", I replied, and burst into tears.

She was right. It was like I only realised right then how exhausting my pace had been: not just in my schedule, but in my head. I put my bags down in my little dormitory room, went to make some tea in the simple communal kitchen, and walked out into the garden. I was fragile, I was messed up, I was finished.

As I looked wearily around me, I saw a small wooden sign stuck in the flower bed. It said...

"Be still, and know that I am God." – Psalm 46:10

I don't know what your name is for that sense that there is something bigger than us, or how you've experienced divine intervention. But for me, in that moment, something incredible happened. It was like God had just whispered into my ear.

Be still. Stop running. Stop pushing. Slow down. Know that I am God. Remember who I am. Remember who you are.

Everything for me had been about what I did.

It was about doing, not being.

It was about doing, not knowing.

I had been pursuing performance, and in that moment, I was given an alternative.

The pursuit of presence.

Not only God's presence, but being present to my own life, to the people in front me. I had to decide whether I was going to give my life presence, or performance. I had not learnt, but would soon discover, that you simply cannot give presence at pace. You have to accept the invitation to be still, as this ordinary little wooden post reminded me.

The phrase "be still" is an English translation of the Hebrew word "raphah". Raphah means to cast down, to let fall, to let hang down, then to be relaxed, slackened, especially the hands. It is used to speak of not making an effort, not exerting yourself. To raphah is to abate, to cease, to fail. It can even mean to be weak.

Now, with "Raphah" tattooed on my right forearm, I am reminded not to go through life white-knuckled.

Raphah, Jess.

Loosen your grip.

Slacken your wrists.

Be still.

I have to choose to unclench my jaw, drop my shoulders, and let go. When I don't raphah, without me noticing at first, life slowly starts to get out of control and then I get stuck in a cage again.

I've seen this with my wildlings. From the time they were little, my boys have loved to wrestle each other. But there is a point where the rough play crosses the line and someone loses their cool. One of them sees red, goes bonkers, the other retaliates, and all hell breaks loose. I'm pretty sure our neighbours think we're absolute parenting deviants because of these wrestles-turned-warfare they overhear. The boys get so mad that they don't hear me or see me or notice that it's out of control.

Someone suggested that when this happens, I get a whistle and blow it and shout "STOP AND DROP!" So I did. It stops them in their tracks and demands an instant reaction. In fact, the boys know that if I say "STOP AND DROP!", anything that happens afterwards is going to be extremely unpleasant for them.

Raphah is like stop and drop.

Stop performing. Stop striving.

This is so opposite to our culture. Our "being" becomes too confused with our "doing". We pour ourselves into our work, into filling our diaries and time with busy activities. We rush from one place to the next, we say yes to every request or demand made of us. Being stressed is like a badge of honour. Being busy is a status symbol. And what this word raphah tells us to be, is the exact opposite of this, which is why I have to look at it every day.

While on that silent retreat, I did my first labyrinth walk. A labyrinth is not a maze, which is a puzzle to be solved – although labyrinths are wonderful to walk through when you're feeling puzzled. A labyrinth is a path that moves from the outside to the inside of a circle, doubling back on itself and circling in and around in a specific pattern. The idea is that you can walk mindfully and meditatively, just following the path without thinking where to go but being aware of your thoughts as you move from the outside of yourself to the heart of the circle. It's very centering.

This was very new for me. My spirituality had always been focused on song and Scripture, but very little silence. I never knew how thirsty I was for this in my soul. Like me, many people are intimidated by silence, perhaps because it can be so awkward. Silence can cause you to address issues that you might be running from. It's easy to fill each day with busyness and then block out concerns through hours of mind-numbing Netflix binging or scrolling on our phones til our thumbs cramp up. None of these activities are bad in moderation but they are not truly restorative and can take the place of truly restful practices, like meditating, walking outdoors or literally just sitting and doing nothing.

Quieting the mind requires practice. Meditation is a powerful way to shut up thoughts that don't serve us. If you're from a Christian background, you may be wary of meditation and silence because it can seem quite "whooo-whooo". Like maybe you're picturing a seated figure in a trance on a cliff facing a sunset with a rainbow over her head. That's not meditation. That's an Instagram post.

Meditation is practiced by such a diverse range of faiths and followers, and I was late to the party on the version of this that resonated with my Christian background. I went on to discover followers of Jesus had been meditating for thousands of years – not with the intention of emptying oneself, but filling oneself with awareness of God. In fact, the original Latin for meditation, is the word "meditatio". Meditatio means "to chew", like a cow chewing the cud. I discovered that silence made space for me to "chew" on essential truths from ancient Scriptures, turning them over and over, extracting all the goodness and nutrition and life that is them.

Even if you feel uncomfortable with the idea of meditating, it is a tried and tested way to sate your soul with silence. It is a practice that helps us to pursue presence, not performance.

Pursue presence, not performance.

My second tattoo is also a word. On my one arm is Rapah, but on my other is Yada.

Yada is translated as "to know" in English, but it's an interesting Hebrew word because we don't really have an exact equivalent in English. The knowing referred to here is to know something intimately, like when you know someone you're related to, your kinsfolk, your family. It even has the intimacy of a sexual relationship, where you know someone fully, nothing hidden. Throw back to the old English phrase, "He ***knew*** her in the Biblical sense". In other words, they doinked their bits together.

It's not factual knowledge.

It's not conceptual knowledge.

It's experiential knowledge.

Like, I can know about Taylor Swift, but I don't really know Taylor Swift. I can know all the lyrics to a Taylor Swift song and have read the backstory to every album and watched the documentaries, but until I have sat in small, intimate gathering of say eighty people at a secret gig where she plays and then asks me to come up, sing with her and be her best friend...well, you get the picture. Although I am very available to do all of the above should the opportunity arise because she is awesome and I have always been a closet teenager and always will be.

Ok, back to meaningful deep stuff. (Love you, T-Swizzle.)

Yada speaks of intimacy, of familiarity, of discovering.

Yada means to discern something, to discover it and experience it deeply.

It's the knowing of a relationship, not facts.

A lot of people think a spiritual life is knowing ***about*** God, or the Divine, or Love, and then doing good things. But I believe a spiritual life is about knowing God, or the Divine, or Love and then just being. Not even being good, just being.

I don't want to be someone who thinks they know everything – which is very tempting for me. I don't want to be someone who pursues knowledge that isn't actually transforming me. Looking down on my arm, seeing Yada tattooed there, reminds me that I want to pursue presence. Being present to God, my world and the people in it – that is what I want to pursue.

As painful as that season of burnout was, it was also a turning point for me. I will always have to watch that part of my personality – where passion blurs into ambition, or where people's opinions become my reward. But if I go back to practicing disciplines that are the opposite of my personality – silence, solitude and mindfulness – I am able to reorient myself to the message tattooed on my arms.

Raphah. Yada.

Pursue presence, not performance.

# KEY 6:
## PURSUE PRESENCE, NOT PERFORMANCE.

Are you trying to pursue perfection?

What expectations do you feel you have to meet?

Are you trying to outperform your imperfections?

What mistakes are you trying to avoid?

When last did you practice silence and solitude?

# CHAPTER THIRTEEN
## HOW TO BE A BETTER PARENT

Dear Parent,

You might be thirty-something-ish. You may have a child or two under the age of four. Even if not, you never knew you could feel so much love, but you also never knew it was going to be this hard.

There are moments of sheer delight, but they're often separated by long, mundane hours that range from busy to infuriating. You feel guilty that you miss your pre-parent life. You wish you didn't lose your temper as often as you do. You know your spouse is supposed to be on the same team as you but often they feel like The Enemy. But most of all, there is this nagging suspicion that you are messing it up.

Parenthood.

Your Child.

Marriage.

Life.

You used to feel like someone who could manage stress, who knew how to handle, who had a game plan. But between discipline and diet, health and safety, tantrums and tiredness, you're just not sure anymore. Not sure you can do it. Not sure that you have what it takes. You're not even sure what exactly you're supposed to do when your three year old throws their cereal across the room and breaks the bowl and now there's glass everywhere and you lose your temper and you're already late for work and you're not supposed to give hidings and you are supposed to be calm and now they're going to be hungry at school and neither of you are going succeed in life.

The End.

If you're not sure what the next right thing is, how can you be sure you'll do it properly?

You are not alone.

I remember when I realised how many of us were in this space. From friends who confessed their behind-the-scenes stories, to my own sit-on-the-kitchen-floor-and-clench-my-fists-and-hit-the-tiles moments. I couldn't help but wonder why it seemed like so many of us are struggling?

I asked my dad. I asked him about his childhood. I asked him about raising us. I asked him why he thought so many parents in our generation find parenting so difficult. Was it like this for you, Dad?

What he said was profound.

He said he thinks our expectations are too high.

He said he thinks we're not used to saying "no" to ourselves.

When we either don't achieve the standards we think we should, or we don't have the luxuries we used to have, we freak out. Whether it's anger, or guilt, or desperation, we assume it's so hard because we're doing it wrong.

This really hit home for me.

Our expectations are too high.

He told me how when he and my mom had kids, they just knew they weren't going to go out and socialise that much anymore. It was a given. It was normal. He observed that for myself and my peers, we generally tried to keep our lives as close to what they were pre-kids, while he seemed to think that for them – well, they basically just lowered their expectations of life.

Interesting theory.

I started to think about it. And I came up with some reasons why I think he may be right.

The first one is that we like to think we "won't let our kids change us". I know I was guilty of thinking this way. I saw other couples with kids change, and "give in", and "lose themselves" to parenthood.

Being the inherently selfish and somewhat naive person that I am, I had decided I wasn't going to "let my children change who I am".

Come on. How many of you said something like that? We set out on a mission not to let our post-baby life look different from our pre–baby life and it just doesn't work. We drive ourselves crazy trying to be the same people, have the same lifestyle, and do the same stuff when everything is different.

The second reason I think my dad is right is that we've been told we can have it all. As a resourced, privileged woman, I've experienced opportunities that were not as readily available to previous generations. Education, career, travel, domestic help, hands-on husbands. But along with those privileges, comes the assumption that it's a realistic possibility to Work Hard and Play Hard and Parent Well and Partner Well all at the same time and equally brilliantly. We assume there are people out there getting this right and if you aren't, well, what is wrong with you? The reality is that for generations before us, (and it continues to be so for many women around the world) if you worked hard, you couldn't spend a lot of time with your kids. If you had kids, you never socialised like you used to. If you weren't working, you had less money. But we're told we can have it all.

Finally, I think we struggle because there is so much information. The irony of putting this sentence in a book has not escaped me, but it's true. We can read any number of parenting books and blogs, and we're exposed to so many models and theories and suggestions that we have a million ways to know we're not good enough. I'm so grateful for the resources that have helped me, but in every article and on every page there is something I'm not doing right. Now I know all about it. I know every time I do something wrong and how it will inevitably scar my child for life. I miss the days when ignorance was bliss.

I certainly don't want to diminish the effort, love and attention you give to your kids.

But seriously, dearest fellow human.

Lower your expectations.

Or alternatively, you could go Google how to be a better parent and do All The Things listed on all the blogs and chat about it at Wine Club, and write a blog post, and start a Pinterest page on dealing with children's sensory development and go on a parenting course and start another small business to earn more money so you can send them to a better school and also stop fighting with your husband. Or you could lower your expectations.

Excuse me, Jess, a question. Could you go too low with your parenting standards?

Why, yes, thank you for asking.

I might refer to the time I was informed by a perfect stranger in a public place that I was a terrible parent. My two year old had shouted at her one year old in a play area, and she stormed away in tears with a lot of words to say at me. Her husband even phoned the restaurant later that day.

Which was weird.

Obviously, I over-analysed the incident. Because when a woman you have never met and knows nothing about you gives you such a thoughtful, unasked for, astute observation like "you're a terrible parent", you have to take it seriously. Even after thinking about our remarkable, constructive conversation for three days, I was still unsure.

Am I a terrible parent?

Or did she catch me on a good day?

In my quest for truth and with a heart to help all the other flailing failures out there who call themselves parents, I have developed this helpful quiz which will assess your answers and evaluate whether you are also a terrible parent.

I highly recommend it, so that when you are lambasted by a strange woman you can calm the situation down by providing her with scientific evidence that she is right.

This quiz should really help you figure out if your expectations are too high, or too low, or somewhere in the middle.

***

## QUIZ: ARE YOU A TERRIBLE PARENT?

Select the answer that **mostly accurately reflects** your response to the question.

1. ARE YOU CURRENTLY A PARENT?

A) Yes.
B) No.
C) Not yet, but this quiz will play a significant role in my decision to be one.
D) None of the above.

2. YOUR THREE YEAR OLD IS HAVING A TANTRUM IN A SHOP BECAUSE YOU REFERRED TO HIM BY HIS REAL NAME AS OPPOSED TO HIS PREFERRED NAME, "SPIDER-MAN". DO YOU...

A) Quickly assemble a Calm Down Corner in the check-out line so he can use sensory-calming activities to self-regulate before labelling his emotions?
B) Start looking around frantically and say, "Does anyone know where this poor child's mother is?"
C) Ask the judgy-looking woman staring at you what she would do?
D) None of the above.

3. AFTER YOUR FIFTEEN MONTH OLD OPENS THE CUPBOARD AND BRINGS YOU A BOX OF CEREAL, YOU DEDUCE THAT HE IS HUNGRY AND IT'S TIME FOR A SNACK. DO YOU...

A) Pop out to the vegetable garden to pull out some home-grown carrots and quickly bake an organic carrot-quinoa-raisin bar for him?

B) Take him to McDonald's because you remember that every meal should have the five food groups in? (Nuggets=protein, chips=carbs, apple juice=fruit, tomato sauce=vegetable. Wait. That's four.)
C) Hide pieces of bread around the house and encourage him to forage for food so you can foster independence and self-sufficiency?
D) None of the above.

### 4. YAY! IT'S POTTY TRAINING TIME. IN ORDER TO GET YOUR TODDLER OUT OF NAPPIES AND USING THE TOILET, YOU DECIDE TO...

A) What nappies? He's been using elimination communication since he was eight months old.
B) Buy the "Toilet Time is Fun Time" app for your child's iPad, and purchase the Infant iPad Holder so it doesn't fall in the loo while he uses it.
C) Ask all your friends who don't have kids what you should do.
D) None of the above.

### 5. ANOTHER MOM ACCUSES YOU OF BEING A TERRIBLE PARENT AFTER YOUR TWO YEAR OLD SHOUTED AT HER ONE YEAR OLD IN THE PLAYGROUND. YOUR FIRST RESPONSE IS TO:

A) Follow her to her car apologising profusely and suggest that you attend a conflict-resolution workshop along with your feuding toddlers.
B) Take a photo of her car while she drives away and shame her online.
C) Offer to start an online crowdfunding campaign for the future therapy sessions she and her child will need.
D) None of the above.

## RESULTS:

### IF YOU SELECTED MOSTLY A'S:

You are indeed a terrible parent. You have good intentions, but most of the strategies you are using are certainly going to cause your child long-term damage. We suggest you read some more Huffington Post articles about parenting and set aside a child-free weekend to strategise a new approach to your children's upbringing. Don't forget – if you make a single mistake, you will probably ruin your children for life. Good luck!

### IF YOU SELECTED MOSTLY B'S:

You are indeed a terrible parent. You have good intentions, but most of the strategies you are using are certainly going to cause your child long-term damage. We suggest you read some more Huffington Post articles about parenting and set aside a child-free weekend to strategise a new approach to your children's upbringing. Don't forget – if you make a single mistake, you will probably ruin your children for life. Good luck!

### IF YOU SELECTED MOSTLY C'S:

You are indeed a terrible parent. You have good intentions, but most of the strategies you are using are certainly going to cause your child long-term damage. We suggest you read some more Huffington Post articles about parenting and set aside a child-free weekend to strategise a new approach to your children's upbringing. Don't forget – if you make a single mistake, you will probably ruin your children for life. Good luck!

## IF YOU SELECTED MOSTLY D'S:

You are indeed a terrible parent. You have good intentions, but most of the strategies you are using are certainly going to cause your child long-term damage. We suggest you read some more Huffington Post articles about parenting and set aside a child-free weekend to strategise a new approach to your children's upbringing. Don't forget – if you make a single mistake, you will probably ruin your children for life. Good luck!

# KEY 7: LOWER YOUR EXPECTATIONS.

What did you say before you had kids that created unrealistic expectations for you?

If you don't have kids, what external narratives have shaped the expectations you do have?

How much do you compare your behind-the-scenes to someone else's highlights reel?

Do you need to limit your exposure to how others approach life, whether it's parenting, body image or lifestyle?

Also, lighten up.
The main thing you should learn from this quiz is stop taking yourself so seriously.

# CHAPTER FOURTEEN
## WHY I LOVE MY STOMACH ROLLS

The problem with doing yoga is how often I am forced to stare at pools of sweat gathering in my stomach rolls.

There's a pose that has me sitting down, folded over, head hanging into my lap, looking at my belly. I don't know what this yoga pose is actually called. Probably Folded Moon or Curled Up Squirrel or something like that. It's pretty gross.

As you know, exercise – or "sportsing" as I like to call it – has never really been my jam. After the failed attempt to break any swimming records, my gym contract was cancelled. Even though I used to go into the gym, swipe my card and leave straight away so I still got free parking, it wasn't enough to keep it going. Gyms are the worst. Gyms are like nightclubs except the lights are on and everyone is sober.

I've tried running, but I've realised that the only thing that can make me run is if someone is chasing me. When I used to try jogging around the neighbourhood, I would only run if I saw a car. Not because I thought someone would chase me, but because it might be someone who knew me, so I would step it up and prance along sprightly so it would look like I'm a super fresh runner lady. Then I'd bend over my knees gasping for air as soon as they turned the corner. I should have run in peak traffic hours – maybe that would have worked.

Tom, on the other hand, is one of those obstacle-course-racing, cross-fitting, trail-running types. He has more shoes than I do, because all of the above require different footwear. He also likes to eat kale and chia seeds, which I'm still convinced is not-real-food. To give him some credit, he does make a killer smoothie that tastes so good I don't even know that the aforementioned not-real-food is in it. He also has a smoking hot body, which personally I don't have any objections to.

The problem with my non-sportsing life is that after two little kids and too many rusks, I don't like the way my body feels anymore. I don't like how breathless I get after playing three minutes of soccer with my boys. I particularly don't like how my four year old can outrun me on the beach, which is problematic when he's running away from me stark naked, throwing his head back laughing and won't come back no matter how much I shout. True story. I don't like it when I'm waving at another mom in the school parking lot and all I can feel is my chicken-wing arm-flab flapping around.

So I started doing yoga. I love yoga. There is no pumping dance music telling me to put my hands in the air like I just don't care. Instead, there is a strong, beautiful woman telling me to breathe, and who never shouts at me when I randomly fall over. I love not wearing exercise footwear that costs more than my kids' school fees. I love that there is always someone in the class who is more bendier than me, and also someone who falls over before me. I am not the worst, which is a refreshing change from the other sportsing I've done. I love that it's a class so you have to actually go at specific times and people watch you so you don't just lie in the corner and have a nap which is what I would rather do. I only did that once, and it was by mistake, because the last pose of the session is one where we all lie down and relax, and I woke myself up with a snoring snort. I do think there's a market there for some entrepreneurs: a napping centre disguised as a gym for moms.

There is something else yoga has given me that I love even more. As I bend over into the Wilted Flower pose or whatever it is that has me navel-gazing, I look at my folded, wrinkled body, squishing over itself and dripping sweat, and do you know what I realise?

I love my squishy belly.

This belly held the two most beautiful gifts in my life. It brought both of my gorgeous, energetic, hilarious boys into the world. This belly isn't hard, flat or ripped but you know what? I've eaten a lot of really, really, good food. I am privileged enough that food is more than survival for me, it's a source of joy, beauty and creativity. I have relished delicious meals with fantastic people. I've laughed until my stomach aches in kitchens, around dinner tables, and over braais. (A braai is what Americans call a barbeque except much much better.)

A friend once told me you have to hunt for the good, and every now and then when I'm feeling sorry for myself, or overwhelmed at some of the repetitively difficult situations I find myself dealing with, and especially when I start worrying and catastrophising my children's future, I have to remind myself to hunt for the good. Hunting for the good makes me grateful, and gratitude gives me perspective, and perspective helps me to get over myself.

No matter how ordinary a day is, or even stressful, something beautiful is hiding away in it like a treasure waiting to be found. Something to be grateful for. Some days, when I open my eyes, I literally have to tell myself that today I will hunt for the good. Even when I am opening my eyes ridiculously early on a day that goes a little something like this...

***

## 4.00 am

"MAMA! I'm awake! Look, it's a morning! What's today?"

Stumbling out of bed, I switch on the kettle. One bottle of rooibos tea with honey, one bottle of formula, one cup of green tea. The boys and I lie on the couch sipping on our beverages of choice, while I play "This Little Piggy went to Market" on the two year old's toes. It's like one of those stock photos of the perfect family.

### 4.07 am

"MY car! "MY car! "MY car!"

The negotiations begin. About 87% of my day is spent negotiating between two small humans with very undeveloped brains.
If you want your brother's car, find him another one you can swap with.
Sorry, boy, you can't have Salticrax for breakfast. Cereal or oats?
No, you cannot go to school naked.

These are just a few things I find myself saying fairly regularly. It becomes quite difficult to know what's sinking in. But, every now and then, I realise that they actually do hear what I'm saying. Like when the four year old and I were playing "Good Guys, Bad Guys" and after he put me in jail, he told me "Sit here, and you can't come out until you control yourself." It would appear someone ***has*** been listening.

Insert here school runs, snack time, nap time, wrestling matches to get nappies changed, running races to get noses wiped and a trip to the homeopath.

### 4.00 pm

"MY truck! MY truck! MY truck!"

### 4.07 pm

"MAMA! I'm hungry. Look, there's a moon. What's for supper?"

Same tune, different words. In the next twenty minutes, I clean up the two year old's swimming costume that has been pooped in (the kind that zips all the way up to the neck), I grab a runaway bottle of Domestos out of the four year old's hand and scoop up an entire tub of yoghurt that was chucked on a suede couch from a highchair. Note to prospective parents: ***suede couches have their origins in the pit of hell.*** **Do not buy one.**

## 4.57 pm

Our evening routine starts with the celebration of Dad's arrival home – dancing, tears of joy and leaping into his arms.

The kids are usually quite stoked to see him, too.

The double pram is loaded up with bikes and skateboards as we meander around the block, and our arrival back at the gate is usually announced by the four year old's meltdown. The stick we found earlier is too short, or the pants he's wearing are too orange, or his brother keeps looking at him. Being four years old at 5pm in the afternoon is difficult. So is being one of our neighbours, I would venture to guess.

Dinner (left overs).
Bath (bubbles, of course).
Bed (finally).
Another bottle of rooibos tea, another bottle of formula and one spilled bottle of Panado.

## 7.23 pm

Did somebody say "wine"?
Yes, please.

***

It's the ordinary day after day after day, at the end of which I collapse into bed with achy feet, wondering if I'll ever not be tired again. However, something happens when I lie there in the dark and think back over the day, deciding to hunt for the good. Gratitude starts unfolding as I remember the other moments.

Like how the four year old told the cashier at the shops his new joke.

(What do cows do on a Friday night? Go to the mooovies.)

Or how the two year old earnestly says "Hi, guyth!" with his adorable lisp to everyone we walked past.

I remember how the four year old makes his cross-eyed funny face to get his brother to stop crying, or how the little one hides under the table and squeaks while we all look for a mouse in the house. I hear the echoes of a little voice whisper, "I love you bigger than the whole world, Mama" and can still feel two smooth, squashy little arms hugging my neck at bedtime. When these two kids laugh, when the four year old tells me a story, when the two year old runs up to me and grabs my legs and throws back his head to look into my eyes, I melt inside. I melt with love, and gratitude, and the realisation that I am privileged and honoured to have these gorgeous children entrusted to my care...every ordinary day.

As Tom and I lie in bed at night, exhausted, grumpy and each convinced we work harder than the other, we start to talk about our kids. About how smart and funny and cute they are, about how much we love them. Sometimes we actually want to go wake them up and play with them. This is usually the sign that we are crossing over into post-traumatic delirium and really need to sleep, so it's lights out and eyes closed.

Did I say this was a pretty ordinary day?

I meant it was another beautiful ordinary day.

Hunting the good turns the pretty ordinary into the beautifully ordinary.

Even though I don't like the sportsing or waking up at 4 am,

I'm glad I found yoga and hunting for good, because together they have given me gratitude. I'm grateful for exercise and my health. I'm grateful for food and family. Yoga even made me grateful for my sweaty stomach.

I'm basically a yogi now, guys.

Namaste.

# KEY 8:
## HUNT FOR THE GOOD.

What are triggers that make you feel sorry for yourself?

Can you hunt for something good in those situations?

Hunt for the good in the last 24 hours.

# CHAPTER FIFTEEN
## THE RAGE CAGE

Tom loves to monitor and track all aspects of his life. He has all kinds of apps on his phone – it tracks how many steps he took, how many hours he worked, and how much money he spent. But, when he first started tracking sleep, I almost killed him. Our boys were babies at the time, and I was getting up two or three times a night to feed. I didn't know how many hours of sleep I'd had – but we'd wake up in the morning and Tom would check his app and say, "Ah nice. I had seven hours of uninterrupted sleep, with three and half hours of deep sleep – look how the graph dips here! Such a deep, deep sleep."

And the rage would just start to boil inside my head and I would launch into wild sleep deprived psycho mom mode. Can your tracker monitor how many times I'm going to punch you in the nose?

Unfortunately, we're taught to monitor so much about our lives. But not our hearts. Our heart is the part of us that gets broken in Grade 9 when she says "let's just be friends", our heart is the part that wants to kill the kid on the playground who tells your child she's not allowed to play with them, our heart is what fills with nostalgia when you hear a song that reminds you of days gone by.

Now I want to reassure you. I am very, very good at being nice. I have been practicing being nice for a long time. When you're a pastor's kid, or a pastor's wife, or a pastor yourself, being nice is what keeps a roof over your head. No matter what your story is, we are all good at being nice on the outside, even when things inside are actually a wreck. Everyone, to some extent, can keep their behaviour socially appropriate even when they are imploding on the inside. It doesn't mean you're free from the rage cage.

One of the reasons that we implode is because of unresolved anger. Behind all the huffing, puffing, ranting, raving, brewing and stewing is the most basic of human experiences: we just aren't getting our way. A few years ago, I read a book called ***Enemies of the Heart*** by Andy Stanley. He explained that the root of anger is the perception that something has been taken from you. Then, a debt-to-debtor relationship is established. Something has been taken, and so somebody owes you.

This wasn't a lightbulb moment for me. This was a strobe light in your face moment for me. Something had been taken away from me. This is why when we had babies, the sleep deprivation made me so mad. I wanted to sleep. I was not getting sleep. I was getting angry. So I would hoot at the person who was driving too slowly on the highway, or I would rev up about someone at work who didn't hear my perspective at a meeting. I would snap at Tom when he forgot to take out the rubbish on a Tuesday morning. I would bark at my mom for giving me unsolicited advice.

Or, there's the time I was on my way to my in-laws' house after church on a Sunday when a BMW came riding up behind me, trying to aggressively pass me. When I flipped him the bird, showing him in no uncertain terms what I thought of his driving, he pulled up next to me, and slowing down he rolled down his window and raised his eyebrows.

"Nice one, Jess." said the husband of my husband's personal assistant as I dropped my middle finger back onto my lap with big eyes.

Apparently, sometimes the pastor's wife is not ***that*** nice.

Anger is a result of not getting something we want, whether it is something we deserve or not.

Maybe you're a woman who has been working hard for a promotion, but it was given to the guy who plays golf with the boss. You're angry and now somebody owes you.

Or perhaps it's a kid whose dad ran off with another woman – taking his childhood with him. The family life this boy wanted was stolen. Now somebody owes him.

What about the man looking for work day in and day out, wanting the dignity of providing for his family but there's no job? He's angry, and somebody owes him.

**Show me an angry person, and I'll show you a hurt person.**

Haven't we all said, or at least felt, you owe me an apology? When we hurt, we feel like someone owes us something. But so often, this perceived debt is one that practically, realistically can never be paid. That's why so often anger is the cage. We are locked in and trapped by a debt that will never be paid. We are stuck.

Think about that overlooked career woman. The promotion has gone to someone else – and even if he wanted to, the woman's boss can't give it back to her. Or how does a dad who left his family pay back his son for a missing childhood? What can possibly be done to fulfill that debt? For the unemployed man, even if he gets a job, can anyone take him back in time and remove the pain of not being able to feed his kids day after day?

When someone owes you something that can never be repaid, you become indebted to something that cannot happen. You become a slave to unresolved anger, a victim that cannot be compensated.

Eventually, if anger stays lodged in your heart for long enough, you start to believe that everybody owes you, not just the person who actually hurt you. In fact, extremely angry people have already decided you won't get it right before you even try.

I know what you're thinking. You're thinking of someone who needs to read this. You're going to take photos of this chapter and send it to them.

But what if that person is ***you***?

I know I'm starting to hold grudges and believing I'm the

victim when I start having imaginary conversations in my head.

Like this completely hypothetical example that never happened a million times...

Me: ***(Stomping around the kitchen, moving things but not actually tidying up, talking under my breath)***

"Sure. Sure, Tom. You sleep in after NOT waking up last night for the boys and I'll do everything in this house. Oh look, the rubbish needs to be taken out. Why don't you have a shower while I handle it again?"

Tom: ***(Walks through whistling cheerfully, leans in to hug me, and becomes aware of my muttering.)***

"Hey babe, shall we...wait, are you okay? Are you cross with me?"

Me: ***(jaw clenched, big sigh, rolled eyes.)***

"No, Tom. I'm tired. Why do you always think I'm cross with you when I'm tired? It's not always about you, you know."

I wish we had a heart monitor we could link to an app that would warn us when we're stacking up anger and racking up debts owed to us. I would love to get a prescription for a "now you can be vulnerable and receive feedback without getting defensive" pill that I could take every morning. While we wait for those to be developed, the next best thing is to ask our friends and family. They know. They notice if there is resentment and anger lurking and lurching out every now and then. If we ask them, they can help us monitor our hearts. The challenge comes with the answers we receive.

When I was still in my early twenties, I had a very rude and know-it-all colleague. She once gently pulled me aside and told me she'd noticed that I seemed to be revving up into the red zone very easily. She had the nerve to tell me that she'd seen a pattern of how I behaved defensively and overreacted at work. It was ridiculous. I was livid that she had the audacity to tell me my emotions were getting the best of me in meetings and tough conversations. She told me it was like I was a car that went from 0 – 100 km/h in a few seconds, and she described how I supposedly jumped to conclusions and wasn't listening. I can't remember everything she said but if I felt like there was a volcano brewing in me as tears welled up in my eyes. I wasn't angry. I was HURT. So before she could say anything else, I stood up, told her she was wrong and walked away.

I'm embarrassed to say the irony of this conversation only hit me a few years later.

I never knew why I was angry all the time, but I did find out there's only one antidote for my anger. There is one thing I could do that would unlock that cage and set me free, and the good news was that I didn't need anyone else to do it. I didn't even need to download an app. The key was already in my hands.

It's forgiveness. The key to the rage cage is forgiveness.

We tend to think that forgiveness is letting the bad guy off the hook, letting the crook go free. It's actually about ourselves going free. Because when we forgive, we are free.

Recently, I heard from an old friend of mine. He messaged me late one Sunday night, all the way from Australia, because he wanted to talk about something that had happened sixteen years ago. Back then, we had worked alongside each other on a team, but I'd gone on to lead a project that he'd expected to be responsible for. As we chatted back and forth that evening, he was finally asking me why I hadn't spoken to him about it at the time. He wanted to know how I could have accepted that role and just acted like nothing happened.

At first, I was confused. I had to read the messages a few times in puzzlement. The incident had taken place so long ago and I couldn't remember the order of events, the exact series of conversations or even the timing of how things went down. But mostly, I was caught off guard at how hurt he still was. He was someone I really cared about. I knew there were times I'd been a bull in a china shop, a know-it-all, ambitious young woman trying to prove her worth. But I also knew that I'd thought of us as close, like a brother and sister. How had I missed this painful experience in his life? As he shared, I realised I hadn't known what his expectations were, or what our boss had dangled in front of his nose. I had absolutely no idea his hopes had been shattered. Of course, at the time, I was young and immature so it wasn't surprising to me that I had made mistakes and hurt people. But I also needed him to know that this was the first time I'd become aware of how he felt.

As we unpacked that season and I heard his perspective, I was heartsore for him. Not just because of the pain of that long-gone moment, but because of the pain he still felt. Lying in bed that night, playing back the sketchy, etched memory reel from my twenties alongside that evening's conversation, I realised that the real tragedy was not the misunderstanding. It was that he'd allowed this experience to become a story he lived in for the rest of his life. I saw how this specific disappointment had been the first in a series of events that took his life off the plan he'd had. Something had been taken from him. He was hurt at the time, furious for years and blamed those of us involved for actually shifting his life onto a different track. Now there was a debt to be paid. The problem was he was the one paying the bill. His unforgiveness toward not just me, but everyone involved, had dominated his story for decades. Unforgiveness hadn't affected me. I didn't even know he was upset. Unforgiveness had made him a prisoner.

I've stacked up a lot of debt on my own account, holding myself captive. I owed Tom because I had been so hard on him. I owed my parents for asking for help so often. I owed my kids because I had been so inconsistent. I owed my in-laws for being difficult and intense. I had to forgive myself for losing wedding rings, losing my temper, losing my way. I had to forgive myself for not taking helpful feedback, or for ignoring caring interventions. I was in debt to myself, and I was charging interest on every missed payment.

No wonder I was broke.

I'm still learning to forgive myself for the mistakes – big and small. I don't live inside the rage cage like I used to but if I'm not careful, the exacting, judgemental, ungracious debt-collector *(me)* drags the guilty culprit *(me)* before the judge and jury *(me)* and sends me to the warden *(me)* who locks me up in solitary confinement again *(me)*.

Luckily, someone has the key (*yay for me!*).

Now, most of the time, I decide to forgive myself. When I forget to take the car in for a service, or leave my phone at home, or realise there isn't any milk in the fridge – I decide with prison-break boldness to forgive myself.

Maybe the person you need to forgive is a great person and they don't even know how they've taken something from you. Well, now you have the key instead of them. Maybe they're diabolical, dysfunctional and dangerous. Well, now you have the key instead of them.

Forgiveness is not letting people off the hook, it's letting ourselves out of the state of mind that we're victims.

Forgiveness is not releasing people from accountability or justice – it's releasing ourselves from living our life at the mercy of their decisions.

Forgiveness isn't forgetting, it's moving through the truth that they don't have a hold on us anymore.

When we cancel the debt, we're free. I'll say it again because it sounds so cool, and also because it's true.

The key to the rage cage is forgiveness.

And life outside of that cage is glorious.

Many years ago, I was involved in running a women's retreat and our theme was based on Hafez's wonderful Dropping Keys poem. There were three sessions named Beautiful, Rowdy, and Prisoners. At the end of the weekend, each of those words had a room dedicated to them where the women could go and reflect on their experiences.

Each room was full of creative pictures, experiences, and songs that reflected the themes from the talks given earlier. Our friend Mariana made the Beautiful Room full of flowers, hanging plants, gentle music, delightful art, stunning decor, luxurious spaces to sit. All around this gorgeous room were scented candles and mirrors with Scripture verses and affirmations written on them for the women to read as they gazed into them, reminding them of who they were and why they are beautiful.

Then, my colleague and friend Madz was in charge of the Prisoner Room. She had set up a big metal sliding security gate in the middle of the room, and placed hundreds of keys lying on the floor. The women were given a chance to stand on one side of the gate, reflect on what God was freeing them from, pick up a key off the floor that had a verse or affirmation or prayer on it, then walk through this big door, out of the "prisons" that had held them captive and be free.

From there, they came into my room which was obviously the Rowdy Room. Rowdy is my jam. We had thumping music, a dance-floor, and fancy party dress up stuff. It was all about celebrating their freedom and launching out into their purpose in life with joy. Here we danced, made cha-cha-trains around the room, sang at the top of our lungs, laughed and let our hair down.

Not long after everyone started journeying through the different rooms, an older woman came up to me in the Rowdy Room with tears in her eyes. She said, "Jess, I've just come from the Prisoner Room. And Jess, I'm free. I'm free! When I was sixteen years old, I fell pregnant and my father made me have an abortion. It's been fifty years, and today I forgave. I forgave my dad for making me do that. And now I'm free!"

That sixty-six year old woman danced around the Rowdy Room with the biggest smile on her face, and tears streaming down her face.

He was forgiven.

She was free.

# KEY 9:
## WHEN WE FORGIVE, WE ARE FREE.

Who are you angry with?

What did they specifically take from you?

Where might your anger with that person be showing up in other areas of your life?

Could you decide that they don't owe you anything anymore?

# CHAPTER SIXTEEN
## BEAUTY TIPS

When I was a young mom of two toddlers, I was often approached by many other women who wanted to know the secret to my glamorous look. And by many other women, I mean absolutely no one.

There was a good reason for this. Like how when I ran my fingers through my glossy locks and I thought, "Oh, a hairclip." It wasn't a hairclip. It was dried yogurt.

Then there's the time when I was waiting in line at the clinic for baby vaccinations. I stood rocking my restless infant in the crowded room, with my I'm-so-chilled-even-though-I'm-in-a-germ-infested-clinic face on, and noticed how often I was catching the eye of people in the queue. They smiled at me. I smiled sweetly back at them.

"Hi there," I nodded silently and serenely at them like a character in a movie. "Yes. I am one of those relaxed, go with flow mamas, how are you?" Until about 20 minutes into my stand–up demonstration of awesomeness when a kind elderly woman whispered to me that my fly was down.

So glamorous.

It makes you wonder. What actually makes a person beautiful? Is it her hair or her clothes or her flawless make up? Is it her skinny bum or long legs or the ability to rock the sky-high wedges?

Here's the truth.

You are not beautiful when you are put together and made up.

You are beautiful when you are brave.

Brave is the mom dropping her baby off at daycare for the first time because, whether she wants to or not, she's got to work full-time.

Brave is the single woman going to another work function alone, another dinner with all the couples, and popping the champagne for another friend getting engaged.

- Brave is the woman visiting the fertility clinic each month, waiting for her own good news, and in the meantime throwing a gorgeous baby shower for her best friend.
- Brave is the forty-something empty nester who starts studying for her degree after the kids have left home and is the oldest person in the lecture hall.
- Brave is the career woman applying for that top position, even though all the colleagues she's up against are dudes who went to the same boarding school as the boss.

Beautiful is the woman who is brave.

On 9 August 1956, more than 20 000 South African women marched to the home of the apartheid government, the Union Buildings, in protest against the extension of Pass Laws to women. Pass Laws were one of the more malicious tools of apartheid, controlling the geographical movements of Black people. Your Pass Book determined where you lived, where you worked, when and where and for what reasons you could travel. These laws were designed to keep Black people in their place. Literally.

On the way to the Union Buildings the women sang a freedom song...

*Wathint' abafazi,*
*wathint' imbokodo,*
*uza kufa!"*

*"[When] you strike the women,*
*you strike a rock,*
*you will be crushed [you will die]!"*

When you strike a woman, you strike a rock.

Now that's beautiful to behold.

Your marital status, your ability to produce offspring and the size of your bra is not what makes you a beautiful person. It's your unique perspective and talent and strength that make you beautiful. It's your ability to partner with other men and women in the workplace and in schools and in families and in communities, to put things right in the world and contribute towards the things that really matter, that make you beautiful. Every single one of us can do that.

Being brave sounds great and glamorous, but mostly, it's not. Mostly it is about sharing our stories, showing up to our pain, and asking for help. Which mostly sounds terrible, but also mostly makes our lives worth living.

There is something so liberating about knowing we are not alone – it makes us brave. Whether it's clinging on to your friend in a scary movie, or sending your friend across the playground to tell the boy that you like him, or stumbling through the dark into your parent's bed because you had a nightmare, from young to old we feel braver when we are with someone else.

When I was completely caught off guard by how hard parenting was, one of the lifelines that pulled me through the hardest times has been my friendships with other moms. I am always surprised that other women are also struggling, and it is always a great relief to me to know that I am not alone. I stumbled across this quote somewhere, a long time ago…

"When one is weak, another is strong. When one is conquering mountains, the other can't hold on. If only we had a rope that tied us together, that linked us."

The thing is, we do.

Our rope is our stories.

Storytelling is throwing lifelines that turn into rope bridges, eliminating islands of souls and looping in the lonesome.

What seems like a simple story, is an exercise in becoming

beautifully connected. When we tell stories and ask questions, we build bridges from one person to another, hoping to keep our heart intact. We place trust in other people, flawed as we know they are. No matter the response, the act of asking and telling true things is always beautiful.

If you want to be brave, throw a rope.

Tell your story and discover you are not alone.

But of course, telling a story is hard and sometimes hearing someone else's story is even harder. We have to lean into the pain if we are going to be beautifully brave, and leave legacies of connection and courage. Pain is part of the process of being brave, and as they say, beauty is pain, too. If you remember your first bikini wax, you'll know what I mean.

Mine took place in a salon called Sajna's in Tooting Bec, London. I arrived late one evening after work, took a piece of paper with a number on it from a machine, and joined the rows of women sitting on plastic chairs, all waiting, like me, for the curtain of one of a dozen cubicles to open and go in when someone called their number. Picture renewing your driver's licence, but for a wax of your intimate bits. It was one of the single most traumatising moments of my life, and I know that waxist wasn't having a good time either because she had to call in someone to help her at one point. I'm pretty sure beauty is not supposed to be so painful that you can't ride your bicycle to work for two weeks afterwards.

I know you don't want to lean into pain. When I'm in pain, I want to curl up in my bed, shut out all the noise, and go to sleep. I don't even want to show up to pain, never mind lean into it. Painful was a word I used to describe my first few years of parenting. Never mind, leaning into the pain. I was supposed to be having the best time of life!

One of my least favourite things about being a mom of little ones was when someone said, "Enjoy every moment."

Seriously?

Enjoy *every* moment?

Do you enjoy being woken up every three hours at night?

"Oooh yippee it's 3 am! I'm going to enjoy this moment of walking into the wall because I am literally blind with exhaustion."

I remember hearing my son Luke crying on the baby monitor, and so I picked him up to cradle him back to sleep. It was a minute or two later that I realised I was sitting up in my bed, rocking and holding the corner of the duvet in my arms and Luke was still in his cot.

At one time, we may have believed that life was designed and intended to be painless. We had this notion that life – if we were smart or strong or lucky enough to get it "right" – would be lovely and pleasant and easy. We may still believe it, or if we have accepted it is not so, we may still hope for it. Somehow we've been led to believe that if we make all the right choices, and do things the right way – life will be awesome and we will be happy all the time. When we experience difficulty or pain, we think something must be wrong. We think we must have messed up somewhere. And so we hurry away from pain. We shut down when the painful conversation happens. We distract ourselves with fun or projects or work or whatever series we're binging so we don't think about the pain in our marriage. Or, even worse, we throw away what is painful because if it is so sore and so hard, it must be broken. It must be wrong for us.

The truth is, whether you like it or not, pain is part of life. As mothers, no matter how we gave birth – we know that there is no life without pain. Glennon Doyle says 'Life isn't hard because you're doing it wrong. Life is just hard." Life begins with fist clenching, gut wrenching, ear shattering pain.

My first birth experience involved thirty-six hours of labour, two epidurals – one of which failed – and an emergency Caesarean section. I'm sure you would agree that whatever way your baby arrived in this world – it was brutal. Childbirth is brutal. But, childbirth is also beautiful. We experience joy and love and moments of such excruciating happiness that we don't have words to describe it. As mothers we have actually already experienced that life is brutal, and life is beautiful. It's a package deal.

Here's what happens when we lean into the pain, and it's another lesson from childbirth. Dr William Sears describes the fear-tension-pain cycle. When we feel pain, we become afraid. This fear causes us to tense up. The tension makes the pain worse. As the pain increases, we become more afraid because we know its coming. The anticipation of more pain makes us more afraid, which makes us tense our muscles, which – you guessed it – causes more pain. The way to disrupt the cycle is to lean into the pain. Stop fighting it. Stop resisting it. This doesn't make childbirth easy, it just makes it easier.

When we accept that life is painful, when we stop fighting it, resisting it, when we stop pretending that it's fine when it is not, there is a release.

Lean into the pain. It is brave and it is beautiful, and it makes us feel alive. As Brené Brown points out, "We cannot selectively numb emotions, when we numb the painful emotions, we also numb the positive emotions."

I don't want to numb the beautiful because I chose to numb the pain.

You may not feel beautiful or brave. But, you can decide to tell your story, lean into the pain and ask for help. Or all three. Doing any of these might be the bravest, most beautiful thing you will ever do.

Mothering made me brave in ways I didn't know I could be. I genuinely think that's why it's been the beautiful, exquisite experience that it is. My most precious and most beautiful moments in my life so far have come from this particular journey of parenting.

When my big boy was still little, I lay on his bed with him after a messy, long, hilarious, exhausting day. There in the dark, he snuggled up to me as he slowly fell asleep, lying with his forehead against mine, his warm chubby hand on my cheek.

"Love you, precious mama", he whispered.

I closed my eyes and took a deep breath.
This right here.
This moment.
This is beautiful.
And then, he licked my face.

# KEY 10: BRAVE IS BEAUTIFUL.

What painful experiences have you had recently that you could call brave?

Who could you tell these stories of your bravery to?

What pain have you been avoiding that you could be leaning into?

Is there something that you're keeping others in the dark about?

Who could you have a conversation with about bringing it into the light?

# PART III
## EMPTY CAGES

# CHAPTER SEVENTEEN
## FINDING SEA GLASS

I wonder what adorable little ten year old Jess would say if she bumped into me and my kids down at the skatepark today. My guess is she'd be polite to me, try to make friends with the boys, then get back to riding her scooter, pushing her glasses up her nose and coming up with a plan for everyone to take turns. I'm sure it wouldn't take too long for her to forget that there's a grown up lady sitting over there with her phone.

As for new mom Jess, I'd notice her sitting in the corner booth of Spur Family Restaurant near the indoor play area. She'd be keeping one eye on her two rambunctious kids, typing furiously on her laptop and...wait. Is she drinking white wine with a ***straw***? I'd want to go over and tell her that the days are long but the years are short, and before she knows it her kids won't want to play on plastic jungle gyms anymore. But I'd know she'd write in her blog about how annoying older moms are who have forgotten what toddlers are like. She looks tired and busy.

Today's Jess feels a long way from those moments, but it's really only been a minute. This brings me such hope. I've experienced first-hand how much significant change can happen in a soul over a relatively short period of time. Life outside of the cage is possible and there is still a lot of life out here left to be lived.

I mean, I am like, actually really young. I am actually a Millennial. Which still sounds young because I am still young. ***(Disclaimer: This material is considered to be true and correct at the date of publication, changes in circumstances after the time of publication may impact upon the accuracy*** *of the material).* I am young and I am also not complicated at all about not being young forever.

Discovering I had ADHD at thirty seven years old was a moment of swinging open that rusty cage door and choosing life on the other side of it. Looking back on the hard times and seeing how many keys were dropped for me has made me so grateful.

But...

Sigh.

Amongst the flourishing freedom and gratitude, lurks regret. Because some things are just done and you can't undo them. What do you do when something is broken and it cannot be put back together? Like, your childhood is over and what happened, has happened. Or that secret you never said out loud took place too long ago to try and explain. It's in the past. What can you do? Or maybe it's the sharp, careless words you said that cut someone deep, but what's done is done. You know what your regrets might be. The could-have-should-have-would-have that casts a shadow over the lightness you might be discovering.

They say hindsight is 20/20 vision, but mine isn't. Because to be honest, looking back I see a dark cloud hanging over the past. Rose-tinted glasses gazing ahead at the future mist up with regret. Dew-drops of "what if" clinging to the lenses. Looking back is painful.

When you learn something later in life, about something you've been dealing with all your life, there are a lot of "what if" moments.

What if I had been diagnosed with ADHD when I left high school?

What if I had understood myself better, and been able to combat the lies with the truth sooner, rather than later?

What if I had been doing the right things for my brain when my kids were born – would they have been happier, felt more loved and safe, been screamed at less?

Empty cages are awesome but what happens to all the crap that went down while you were still stuck inside?

I live near a wonderful, wild beach in Westbrook that gets pounded by huge waves all year. It's a rocky coastline with a big shore break that pushes shells, driftwood and all kinds of debris up onto the sand. Since we moved here, I've been collecting sea glass. Green, brown and white pieces of glass that have been washed up on the shore. They were once bottles of beer, or glass jars, broken who knows where or when.

I don't know how long these shards are tossed in the waves and across the rough sand before they look the way they do when I pick them up, but I find them along the shore. Smoothed out edges, misty and opaque, little treasures from something that was broken. They are exquisitely beautiful to me – made by humanity, shaped by nature.

I have jars of them on my windowsills, where they sift the sunlight coming in. Every time I pop down to the beach for a quick swim, or watch the boys have a rumble in the shorebreak or go for a chatty stroll with a friend, I pick up sea glass and bring it home.

One day, after returning from the beach with a handful of sea glass in my pocket, I walked into the kitchen to find that the monkeys had entered our house through an open window and smashed two wine glasses all over the floor. And no, not my own two mischief-makers. It was the little, furry, grey, Vervet monkey troops that cause playful chaos all over our neighbourhood. It was an overwhelming mess with these razor sharp pieces of glass scattered across the floor. I was so irritated and annoyed. I was sweeping glass and picking up shards, trying not to get cut. I was yelling at the kids to stay out of the kitchen, searching for the fine splinters of pieces I'd missed – when I stopped and looked down at these little barbs of glass in my hand. I know this kind of broken. Messy. Dangerous. Painful. Nothing would piece this wine glass back together. What is done is done.

I don't always have these contemplative existential moments in the flurry of real life, but I felt this one. I know what it's like to hold something broken in my hand. I even know what it's like to grip tightly to something that is cutting you, hurting you, bleeding you dry – just because it's familiar.

Looking down at those broken pieces of wine glass in my one hand, and knowing that in my pocket was the sea glass, I felt a whisper of truth. A key to my cage. Yes, Jess, you ***do*** know this kind of broken. This is what broken looks like up close. There is no repairing this mess, this history, this Before. But you also know the sea glass. You know how broken ends up beautiful. Never the same again, but exquisite nonetheless. You have seen the Before, but you've also seen the After. And the After is so lovely in its own way.

Whatever kind of spirituality you practice, I would like to share one that shows up in mine. In Christianity, the mercy, love, and divine assistance from God to humanity is called grace.

Grace is one of the most popular names in my era of parenting. Everyone I know with a girl-child has called her Grace. I don't think you can even be the parent of a girl in the 2000s without bestowing the name Grace on one of your offspring. Think about it. You know I'm right.

Grace is so much more than a popular name, though. Grace is getting to participate in the abundance of God's perfect, divine, eternal love – but getting all of that while you're still just being ***you***. The as-you-are-right-now-you. The normal, quirky, confused, inconsistent you. Grace is experiencing oneness with God when you haven't yet improved, or ascended, or moved on from whatever you are struggling with. Grace is a demonstration of unearned Love. You get it when you don't give it. You can't betray this Love or lose it. You don't create or uncreate this Love. Grace is Love that is not earned through performance or perfection. It is freely offered with no strings attached.

This kind of Love sounds too good to be true because it's so rare in this world – unconditional, unloseable Love. I think that's why Grace puzzles us a bit, but we know it when we feel it. Anne Lamott says: "I do not understand the mystery of grace – only that it meets us where we are and does not leave us where it found us." I find it hard to describe Grace because it's something to "yada" – a knowing of experience, not information.

But if there is only one thing to "yada", it's Grace.

I experience Grace through Christ, so I resonate deeply with what the 11th century Italian mystic, Francis of Assisi, says.

"Above all the grace and the gifts that Christ gives to his beloved is that of ***overcoming self.***" (emphasis added)

Our surrender to Grace is how our Self is overcome and transformed. Love crashes over us like the waves on Westbrook beach, if we will only surrender to its wild, enveloping depths. When the what's-done-is-done part, the irreparable parts, the cutting-cringey parts of our stories are surrendered to the waves of this Love, we are gifted sea glass from glass shards – rough edges smoothed out, sharpness made soft, broken made beautiful.

I've personally seen shattered glass turn to sea glass. I've seen what happens when we bring our brokenness and toss it into the ocean of Goodness and Grace. Not just on beach walks, but in the decades of my broken, beautiful journey with God, whom I know as Creator, Father, Mother, Friend, Christ, Guide, Source, Spirit and Power. And God loves Jess the Mess, not Jess the Best.

Growing up immersed in the Christian world, there was a prayer I had heard so many times I could say it by heart with my eyes closed. Well, I mean, most prayers are said with eyes closed. Whatever, you know what I mean. This prayer is from the Hebrew collection of songs and poems, known as the Psalms and it begins with "***The Lord is my Shepherd, I shall not want.***" Maybe you've heard it at a church service or wedding or funeral, maybe it sounds vaguely familiar or maybe it was one of the first verses you memorised. Right at the end of this famous Psalm, the writer says, "***Surely goodness and mercy will follow me all the days of my life.***"

I've always wondered about that. It's weird. Why would God *follow* you? Especially with goodness and mercy? Every time I heard this I thought, "If I'm going to get some goodness and mercy, I don't need it bringing up the rear. I need it right here and now. Or out front maybe, clearing the way. What are you doing back there, God?"

Goodness and mercy following me seems a waste of a good thing. The only thing I want following me is more people on Instagram.

That day in the kitchen, as I looked down at the broken glass in my hand, I suddenly understood.

This is what God is doing back there.

This is why God has goodness and mercy washing over the wake of my life.

God is transforming broken into beautiful.

Goodness and mercy is what turns glass shards into sea glass.

Standing there in my kitchen, sweeping up broken wine glasses with beautiful sea glass on the counter, I felt like God wanted me to know what was happening in the wake of my ADHD diagnosis.

That, even though behind me lay regret and words that cannot be unsaid, I would one day be able to turn around, look behind me and see goodness there anyway.

When I look back on my university days, or my mothering, or my marriage, yes, there are lots of broken things, regrets or mistakes but there is also a legacy of love.

All of that past.

All of this present.

All of this, washed over and over again in God's goodness and mercy, the ugly mess can be smoothed into something beautiful.

Shattered glass becomes sea glass when covered by Grace.

Could you make space in your worthy, wonderful, wounded heart for a Love that is fond of you the way it finds you?

# LIFE OUTSIDE THE CAGE

What regrets do you carry around with you?

Looking back on your life, where have you experienced rough edges being smoothed out?

Who has shown you unconditional grace, and how have you received it?

How open is your heart to the truth that you are worthy and loved?

# CHAPTER EIGHTEEN
## WE CAN BE BOTH

In July 2021, while the COVID-19 pandemic was flooding South Africa with a devastating third wave, another storm was unleashed. On Sunday night, we went to bed knowing our former President Jacob Zuma had finally been arrested and imprisoned for failing to appear in court to face his many corruption charges. On Monday morning, we woke up to a country on the brink of civilian warfare.

What started out as crowds protesting Zuma's sentence, had evolved into complete civil disorder and looting. Our phones buzzed endlessly and social media was inundated with reports from all over our city and province. We watched videos and listened to voice notes in disbelief as we saw entire shopping malls stormed and looted, trucks and businesses set alight, and entire supply chains and distribution grinding to a halt. Mobs armed themselves to attack and plunder resourced communities who then barricaded their neighbourhoods and organised defensive tactics. It was sickening and terrifying to see buildings burning, hear gunshots fired and watch my husband head out at night on patrol armed only with a baseball bat.

I felt so angry and afraid.

Long after the dust settled, we realised what became known as "The Unrest" was not simply political supporters of Jacob Zuma protesting his arrest or poor, unemployed people who couldn't take the pandemic anymore, but a complex, calculated, tactical move on the chessboard landscape of South African politics. Isn't it always like that? The most volatile, surprising, unexpected situations in our lives are often less random and more complicated than we realise.

While we didn't know this at the time, what we did know was that we were trapped. Trapped in our homes and neighbourhoods without access to food or medical supplies, blocked off from family and friends. This is where the incredible resilience, determined fortitude and agile problem-solving of South Africans rose to the fore. I wish I could show you how we organised ourselves so that people could eat and get medication to those who needed it. I wish I could show you how people patrolled and protected not only their own homes and businesses but came together to save entire communities from violence. I wish you could have seen the crowds that emerged to clean up our city after that week – literally picking up glass and metal and moving burnt cars out of the street.

I felt so inspired and proud.

A few days after the unrest subsided, I was driving home from a massive clean up and rebuild initiative hosted by our church. As I drove past buildings still smouldering, I suddenly started to weep. Could I feel so angry and so inspired at the same time? Could I be so furious with some of my countrymen and so proud of others, too?

I got home that afternoon, and wrote this poem.

WE CAN BE BOTH
BY JESS BASSON

I CAN BE SO RELIEVED THIS IS OVER,
AND SO ANGRY THAT IT HAPPENED.
I CAN BE INSPIRED BY THE PEOPLE'S EFFORTS,
AND FURIOUS THAT PEOPLE DID THIS.
I CAN BE GRATEFUL FOR WHAT I HAVE,
AND GRIEVING FOR WHAT I'VE LOST.
I CAN BE BOTH.
LIMITING MYSELF TO ONLY ONE
LIMITS MY HEALING AND RECOVERY.

I CAN BE STRONG,
AND I CAN BE OVERSENSITIVE.
I CAN BE OPTIMISTIC,
AND I CAN BE OFFENDED.
I CAN BE PLAYFUL,
AND I CAN BE AWARE OF HOW PRECARIOUS THIS IS.
I CAN BE BOTH.
LIMITING MYSELF TO ONLY ONE
LIMITS MY HEALING AND RECOVERY.

I CAN BE CAUTIOUS,
AND I CAN BE KIND.
I CAN HOLD SOMEONE ACCOUNTABLE,
AND I CAN FORGIVE THEM FOR THEIR SINS.
I CAN HAVE SAFE BOUNDARIES,
AND I CAN MAKE GENEROUS ASSUMPTIONS.
I CAN BE BOTH.
LIMITING MYSELF TO ONLY ONE
LIMITS MY HEALING AND RECOVERY.

AND IT'S NOT JUST ME.
IT'S WE.
WE CAN BE ANGRY AT THOSE WHO TOOK FROM US,
AND FEEL COMPASSION FOR THOSE WHO HAVE VIOLATED THEIR CONSCIENCES.
WE CAN EXPECT MORE OF HUMANITY,
AND WE CAN ACKNOWLEDGE HOW PEOPLE WHO FEEL DEHUMANISED MIGHT BEHAVE.
WE CAN DEMAND JUSTICE,
AND DECIDE NOT TO JUDGE.
WE CAN BE BOTH.

LIMITING OURSELVES TO ONLY ONE
LIMITS OUR NATION'S HEALING AND RECOVERY.

CHAOS MAKES US CRAVE CERTAINTY.
CERTAINTY MAKES US SEARCH FOR SIMPLE ANSWERS.
SIMPLE ANSWERS REDUCE PEOPLE TO

EITHER | OR
BLACK | WHITE
GOOD | BAD
SUBURB | TOWNSHIP
LOOTER | PATROLLER
RICH | POOR
PROTESTOR | PROTECTOR
RIGHT | WRONG

MAY WE ALL CHOOSE TO BE
WOUNDED HEALERS.
BECAUSE REMEMBER,
MY NEIGHBOURS KNOWN AND UNKNOWN,
WE CAN BE BOTH.

***

I share this with you because when we name our cages and find our freedom, we need to give ourselves permission to be both. Living on the outside of the cage is not a destination, it's an ongoing process. Like a bird, you may circle back on yourself as you soar. Freedom isn't linear – it's a flowing, living, organic, messy, process of growth.

Life outside of the cage is a dance between Both/And.

Both hurting/And healing.

Both rest/And work.

Both saying sorry/And celebrating progress.

It may feel clumsy at first, but the dance between Both/And is one we all have to learn to do.

As an awkward ten year old, I did ballet to help me with my slouching posture. I remember arriving at ballet straight after swimming practice, dripping like a drowned rat while all the other little girls pranced daintily around the studio in their stockings. I was all skinny elbows and knobbly knees, with my tongue sticking out as I tried to get the positions right. They said I had to stand in the back row because I was "so tall", but I know it was because I was a terrible dancer. While I may suck at ballet, I do have the confidence of a peacock if you play Whitney Houston's "I Wanna Dance With Somebody" because I have spent hours dancing to it in my bedroom. This week.

You might not be good at the Both/And dance yet, but the more you practice the more natural it will feel. You might slip up, but don't give up.

Life outside the cage is full of contradictions and we are never truly done flying out of the cage. But we can be both. Reducing ourselves to one – either trapped or free – will limit our healing because we are never truly done. The soaring, flourishing, free life is not simple or certain but we're more empowered to choose what our response will be to the setbacks or letdowns.

When that cage door opens, and you go soaring out, that's okay. When you find yourself hovering around those familiar old bars, perched precariously on a cage you know very well, that's also okay. When you find yourself in a new season of life with new shiny cages you haven't noticed before, it's okay. We can be both. And if you find yourself back inside a cage again pick up the keys, receive the Grace, and step outside again.

# LIFE OUTSIDE THE CAGE

Can you think of a time when you slipped up and that made you give up?

What thoughts or emotions do you have that seem to contradict each other?

Is there a situation in your life where you need to accept the Both/And?

Notice where you tend to take a few steps forward and then a few steps back.

Can you give yourself permission to work at progress, not perfection?

# CHAPTER NINETEEN
## FREE AS THE BREEZE

Remember how you and I didn't meet at a fancy dinner with the dark chocolate brownies because I never get invited to those? Well, Tom and I eventually went to one. We farmed out the kids to the long-suffering grandparents, and got into our best clothes which in my case, was a borrowed red dress and, for Tom, was his classic formal suit.

We pulled into the parking lot of the gorgeous venue, and as Tom stepped out of the car, we heard the swift, savage sound of his pants ripping from crotch to crack. He froze mid-exit, looked over his shoulder at me in dismay, and we both burst out laughing.

It was not just a tear. It was a giant hole in his suit pants. Tom was as free as the breeze.

Cue a lightning quick visit to the nearest Woolworths department store, privacy preserved by a blanket we found in the boot of my car, and a hilarious jaunt through a crowded mall on a Friday night. One of my personal proudest moments was the two of us pulling back into the self-same fancy venue parking lot only thirty minutes later. I may not be able to run fast, but I can hustle through a mall.

Despite his history with pants, Tom is actually quite a snappy dresser. He used to have a local designer-made T-shirt with a drawing of a birdcage on it. The cage door was wide open, but the bird was lying dead on the floor. It was very cool and obscure and philosophical.

But, it was also very true. Freedom isn't freedom if you don't walk out the door.

It's one thing to have a cage door flung open in front of you.

It's another to actually step through it.

We can have the keys dropped in our hands by a sage.

We may even have the door unlocked and flung wide open.

But how do we actually walk through the door and take off again?

There are no silver bullets, or foolproof plans, or seven magical steps to freedom. But there are truths that help us to break out of cages. For me, one of those is my faith, and my relationship with God.

Sometimes, it's really hard for me to admit that. Because religion is one of the worst prisons people find themselves in. And not just any religion. My own world of Christianity has a truly heart-breaking, shocking and real record of imprisoning people.

Like most of us know, sometimes the source of our greatest joy can also be the source of our greatest pain. The Church is one of those for me. I love her, and I know she's better than that, and she's super messed up sometimes.

Not long after I came home to the shattered wine glass in the kitchen, and had my moment of hope that a legacy of hurt, pain and brokenness could be smoothed out and somehow restored, I was back walking on the beach again.

This time, I was fuming.

I was churned up and worked up, feeling angry and heavy-hearted. I had been having a conversation with a dear, valued friend who had been incredibly hurt by the Church. I felt so responsible for this pain she and so many others had endured – not because I had done anything to her, and not because she held me accountable for it, although she was asking me to advocate for better from within the system. I felt responsible because I want people to find freedom and grace, not religion and rejection. As I quietly despaired, feeling overwhelmed and sad at the damage done and still taking place, I was reminded again of the promise that God's goodness and mercy was following me. Cleaning up. Finding good in the wake of our not good. Not just me, but even the Church.

I don't know if religion has hurt you, held you down, judged you or rejected you. I know it has for so many, and for this – I am truly sorry. I'm sorry for participating in a system that has excluded, enslaved, and manipulated. I'm sorry for not fully grasping this side of my faith's history for so long, and for not always having the courage to speak up when I see the injustices that still take place. There are doors I'm still working up the guts to step through.

The truth is that for me, the door of my cage has often been opened by my interactions and experiences with God. The keys that were dropped were often given to me by wise, loving, gracious people of faith. The messy, marvellous, mixed–up place called the Church was one of my safe places when I was a messy marvel and the Church was the backdrop to so much of my healing. I found my voice on the stage of a church auditorium after I lost it in a church parking lot.

I am not suggesting that you find religion. If you catch a whiff of that fake stuff, run a mile. We're looking for free as the breeze, remember? What I am presenting is the idea that freedom is not only a circumstantial external existence, or a set of psychological modalities, or intentional relational practices – but also a spiritual internal state of being.

I mean, what even is freedom? So many of us have been told that freedom is the right to do or say or be whatever we want as long as no one is hurt. Doing whatever you want to do and however you want to do it sounds a lot like freedom, but as most of us know, it often ends up with us being enslaved again. Freedom is often doing exactly what you ***don't*** feel like doing – like forgiving someone, or asking for help, or hunting for the good when we're grumpy, or exercising.

For me, freedom isn't just being myself again. I'm not sure I'll ever fully be myself – at least not all the time. Freedom isn't overcoming all my obstacles and being able to say I'm okay now.

For me, freedom is knowing I am loved, knowing I am worthy of compassion and having purpose in life, even when I'm not okay.

I am free not because I have overcome all my limitations, but because I know who I am even when I fail.

I am free not because I can now get things right all the time, but because I know that I am loved for who I am, not what I do.

And, I am not even free because I am fulfilling my dreams and doing what I love, but because I have purpose and calling that is about others, not just myself.

When it comes to matters of spirituality, I'm always pleasantly surprised how often we all have different names for the same concept. The Universe, the Divine, God As I Understand God, YHWH, Allah, a Higher Power, Love. In every century on every continent, in every culture and creed there has been a primal sense that there is more out there, that there is a Source or Consciousness beyond us. All these names are an ode to our deep connection to each other that breaks the laws of here and now. They are vast, big, grandiose concepts that there is something beyond time, space, the material and physical. Something bigger than us.

Whatever your name for Something Bigger is, I believe that this grand God is good, that the universe is on a good trajectory. History and science and psychology have proved this: when we zoom out, the universe is headed in the right direction even if, when we zoom in, we still have a long way to go. I also believe that the fingerprint of the Divine is found in the soul of every human. When I started doing yoga and learnt that "Namaste" meant ***"The divine in me recognises the divine in you."***, I nerded out on the wonder and beauty of the phrase. It wasn't far off my Christian origins of ***"God created human beings; he created them godlike, reflecting God's nature."*** (Genesis 1:27, MSG).

I believe that every human is created to bear the image of God – we are good. We were made good, we long for good, we recognise good deep in our DNA and we ache for it now – not in some afterlife but now. One of the things that I love about humans is despite our nonsense we still work for, search for, celebrate, cry and laugh over the good in the world. Whether we find it in our own small victories of finally making sourdough bread, or in a viral video about a guy who saves a kitten from a tree, or shamelessly laugh-crying at the win of the underdog at the Olympics – we were made to instinctively know good when we see it! But the limitless good is so grand and eternal, the mysterious Source of this goodness-imprint – it can feel a little abstract. While the edges of a trillion-something-year-old expanding universe are glorious, I need something a little bit more down to earth as a point of contact.

One of the weirder, more mysterious beliefs of the Christian faith is that Jesus is fully human and fully divine. It's a Both/And. Not half God and half human, there is no meeting halfway here. It's a fully immersive experience. I love this. Partly because I am a big fan of non-binary explanations for things, and I prefer both/and to either/or. But I also love this because I understand Jesus as this point of contact for humanity – where the Infinite chose to be limited by time and space so that the ordinary, working, walking around, making-our-way-through-life people like me could get close up to God. No more "guy in the sky" to figure out, this is an up close and personal encounter.

Following Jesus is how I walked out of my cage. I don't think I would have stepped out if I hadn't found Someone for my soul to follow out. I think I'm smart, privileged, well resourced and curious enough to have walked my thinking, my emotions, and my body out of my cage. I'm just not convinced I would have found my soul with room to breathe, free as a breeze, without finding the God that I knew had walked in my shoes.

Friend, I believe you can do the work, practice the wisdom, and grow into your true self. Just don't leave that mysteriously eternal divinely imprinted part of yourself behind. As you seek your freedom, I want to encourage you to find a spiritual home. It doesn't have to be a church, or a mosque, or an ashram, or a temple. But spiritual vitality is not something to be done alone. Because for a human to become their full self, there have to be other humans there, too. We were made for connection and community. Paging back through my story, I cannot find significant breakthroughs that were not held alongside other flawed but failing-forward friends who shared both my doubts and my faith.

Whether you've been worn out and burnt out by religion, or mostly been skeptically wary, or self-sufficiently indifferent, I believe a spiritual curiosity about your connection to God, in the context of community, is part of the way out.

What does a healthy spiritual community look like? Christians don't have the monopoly on manipulation and madness. Wherever you choose to pursue spiritual growth, choose wisely.

A quick story from my guy, Jesus, that might help. He had some very strong opinions about religious communities, which is primarily why he ended up being handed over by the Temple leaders of his day to the Roman Empire. He didn't like self-serving leadership, and they didn't like him.

Jesus lived in the first Century, in the Ancient Near East which was primarily an agricultural society. When he taught, he told stories. Stories that would make sense to the locals he knew and lived alongside – people who were shepherds, farmers, and working folk in the rural villages that served as centres for everything that goes along with the farming life. (Sidebar: context is everything. This is why, when taken out of context, some of Jesus' conversations with actual real other people sound weird to our 21st Century ears).

Anyway, one of the ways Jesus described himself so that this community could relate to him, was like this:

"Yes, I am the gate. Those who come in through me will be saved. They will come and go freely and will find good pastures. The thief's purpose is to steal and kill and destroy. My purpose is to give them a rich and satisfying life." – John 10:9-10 (NLT)

Obviously I have a penchant for gate and door metaphors. When I read this, I don't see a sheep's pen with a gate, which is what Jesus was probably pointing to as he spoke on some scrubby hillside. I picture a sci-fi movie-like scene of this gloriously, extensive, breathtaking beautiful universal Love expanding beyond time and space, and right in the centre of this horizon-like blast of energy is a gateway, a door, an entrance. One that I'm invited to walk through, and attempt to do daily by following Jesus.

But, in this originally agricultural metaphor, Jesus is not only describing himself, but the way people who follow him look. He's describing what a healthy spiritual community should look like.

First of all, this doesn't sound like religion. Religion keeps people divided – the good guys in, and the bad guys out. Religion is controlling. But Jesus says those who walk through his Door, can come and go freely. They will find wide open spaces, which are flourishing, nourishing places to live. His whole reason to exist, he wants us to know, is to give people thriving, abundant lives. If you're wondering if a community of faith is a good fit for you, you should definitely expect to find an eclectic bunch of misfits. Where there are people, there are problems. But if it's a healthy, growing, gracious group, they will be flawed, but they will be coming and going freely. They will live flourishing, nourishing lives despite their missteps and mistakes. They will have a purposeful, rewarding sense of life – even when life is a hot mess.

Secondly, from my experience, if you do seek out spiritual life in a religious community and you feel like you're being stolen from, if life is being sucked out of you, if there is division and relational brokenness in that community – that's not good. And God is good. When Jesus is talking to these Jewish country folk on the pastoral hills around Galilee, he offers to save them from the version of religion they personally know – which at the time, was a powerful elite who used rules and regulations to keep the people under control, and they did this in conjunction with a powerful empire that used violence and warfare to keep the people under control. They would have wanted to be saved from that, and Jesus offers to do just that through his Way. Jesus offers to free them – not from fire and brimstone, or from hell, or for heaven, like so many of us think. He offers to free them from a life where they feel like they've been robbed, or stolen from or dead inside. That's what thieves do. Thieves are takers. Jesus is a giver.

As you pursue freedom not just for your mental health, your identity, your relationships or sense of self but also for the deeper part of you, hunt for other people doing the same. People not looking for an afterlife, but an abundant life. People not pursuing perfection, but pursuing presence. Look for spiritual communities that believe God is good, that believe that who you are is good, and who don't use manipulation or control to get people to be good. I know from experience that these places and these people do exist.

Freedom isn't freedom if you don't walk out the door.
So make sure all of you is on your way out.

# LIFE OUTSIDE THE CAGE

What experiences have you had with religious communities, and how are those experiences affecting your spiritual growth?

How much attention have you given to your spirit or soul?

Does it feel fully alive?

How are you cultivating curiosity and openness in your spiritual formation?

# A SET OF KEYS

Reach out and ask questions.
Choose honesty instead of hiding.
Say something.
Name it to tame it.
Good choices make great changes.
Pursue presence, not performance.
No excuses. Just exercise.
Lower your expectations.
Hunt for the good.
When we forgive, we are free.
Brave is beautiful.
Grace turns shattered glass into sea glass.
We can be both.
Freedom isn't freedom if you don't walk out the door.

# A BENEDICTION

Dear Beautiful Rowdy Prisoner,

May you find language to name your cage,
and the courage to speak it to someone safe.

May you become aware of the keys that have been dropped
all around you,
and own them because they are now yours.

May you find the humility to ask for help,
and the wisdom to know from whom.

May you find the courage to walk out of the open door,
and remember who you were created to be.

May you no longer see yourself as a small woman,
But join the tribe of imperfectly present Sages,
Ducking our heads because we've grown to tall for those cages,
Standing on each other's shoulders to reach new heights,
Failing forward and catching those who slip with grace.

EMPTY CAGES

# THE END

# APPENDIX: UNDERSTANDING ADHD

According to the Diagnostic and Statistical Manual of Mental Disorders (DSM), there are 18 symptoms of ADHD:

1. Nine symptoms of the **Hyperactive-Impulsive Type.**
2. Nine symptoms of the **Inattentive Type.**
3. The **Combined Type** has at least 5–6 symptoms from the one, and 5–6 symptoms from the other, and often their symptoms are evenly distributed between the two.

An ADHD diagnosis will not only include evaluating these symptoms, but also how long they have been present and how much they are impacting your daily life. There is more to diagnosing ADHD than ticking off boxes on a list, but it is a helpful place to start.

Let's get down to the symptoms of ADHD, starting with the more well–known type.

## HYPERACTIVE-IMPULSIVE TYPE

People with primarily Hyperactive-Impulsive ADHD struggle with (surprise!) impulse control — moving, squirming, and talking at even the most inappropriate times. It's not just physical – impulse control affects their thoughts, opinions and emotions. They are often quick to react, impatient, and interrupt others.

Here are the 9 commonly seen symptoms:

*1. Often fidgets with or taps hands or feet or squirms in their seat.*

My version of this is that my whole life I've reflexively bounced my one knee. I often don't even know I'm doing it until someone gets annoyed enough to ask me to stop. Recently, I was watching a movie with my sister, who paused to ask me if I know that I'm doing "that" with my finger? I had no idea what she was talking about, but apparently I was flicking my index finger up and down. "That" unconscious fidget is often very irritating to people around them, and can get you repeatedly reprimanded.

*2. Often leaves the seat in situations when remaining seated is expected.*

This can look like getting up from their school desk without permission, standing up in meetings, leaving the table without excusing themselves, and might show up in other situations that require remaining in place.

*3. Often runs about or climbs in situations where it is inappropriate.*

This restlessness looks different for adults than children. What is running or climbing in kids, might be disappearing randomly from a social setting for a change of scenery or walking away from a conversation with adults.

*4. Often unable to play or engage in leisure activities quietly.*

Loud. It's true, we are often loud. Just this weekend, we were at a fancy gala dinner and someone found me by following my voice to the back of the room. Loud could also look like humming, whistling, talking, singing, making funny noises with our mouths or even banging stuff around.

*5. Is often "on the go," acting as if "driven by a motor".*

While this one isn't something I personally experience, I've learnt that many ADHD people struggle to be still for extended times, for example in restaurants or meetings; they may be experienced by others as being restless or difficult to keep up with. For adults, this can even be a feeling inside of them that no one else really notices.

*6. Often talks excessively.*

Oh, the shame of oversharing. The inner cringe of realising that you've been dominating the conversation. Realising you're staying on a specific topic for too long, knowing you need to stop but you can't because there are so many more details or interesting things to be said. So many thoughts, so many words.

*7. Often blurts out an answer before a question has been completed.*

I often complete people's sentences, or anticipate what they're going to say. The ADHD brain is often making connections really quickly so we can bust out seemingly unrelated responses, or try to speed things up when someone is being slow and deliberate.

*8. Often has difficulty waiting their turn.*

Waiting is hard for an ADHD brain. We have a form of time blindness, in that we are so in the moment that later feels like a million days away. Waiting in line, or waiting for a reply to an email, or waiting for someone to do something you've asked them to do, waiting for your turn in a conversation. Patience is a neurological challenge, not a character defect for the ADHD brain.

*9. Often interrupts or intrudes on others.*

The ADHD brain often butts into conversations or gives unasked for advice. If I don't watch myself and notice my behaviour, I often find I will intrude into a situation, or take over what others are doing, or dominate a project. Can you see how the Hyperactive-Impulsive ADHD is different for older people and adults? Sometimes, all of this is well-masked by self-control, the expectations of society and years of reigning oneself in, but that in itself is exhausting and failure is frowned upon. ADHD people are usually quite hard on themselves because they know what they're doing is "wrong", but they keep doing it.

## INATTENTIVE TYPE

This is mostly me. People with the Inattentive subtype of ADHD have difficulty focusing, finishing tasks, and following instructions. They are easily distracted, forgetful, possibly daydreamers who may regularly lose track of their belongings, their time or their train of thought or, say for example, their wedding rings.

Experts believe that many children with the inattentive subtype of ADHD may go undiagnosed, especially girls. They're harder to spot because they're less disruptive (especially when they go to weird little distraction-free schools with no auditory overstimulation, hello little Jess!)

Here are the 9 symptoms for Inattentive Type ADHD:

*1. Often fails to give close attention to details or makes careless mistakes.*

Oh, how many times have I read over an email or social media post again and again looking for typing errors only to see one when it's too late? So, so many time. I mean, times. See what I did there? But that's not the biggest problem for me personally. The lack of attention to detail in my brain shows up in that I cannot remember conversations correctly which is very frustrating in an argument. I miss details in emails and let people down. I cannot follow a recipe to save my life. I get the time of my ADHD appointment wrong. It's maddening to the people around me, and it makes me feel like I'm going mad.

*2. Often has difficulty sustaining attention in tasks.*

From remaining focused during lectures to paying attention to conversations, it's hard for an ADHD brain to keep going at one task. I might read an email or text and mentally tell myself to reply to it, but then lose steam if it's a complex reply and move onto something else.

*3. Often does not seem to listen when spoken to directly.*

I've learnt to hide this quite well, but often my mind seems elsewhere, even in the absence of any obvious distraction. It's because what's distracting me is inside my brain, not necessarily in the surrounding environment.

*4. Often does not follow through on instructions and fails to finish chores, or duties in the workplace.*

Follow up and follow through is a real struggle for the ADHD brain. Whether it's actioning an email or meeting a deadline many ADHD brains start what they need to do, then end up losing focus before it's done. I have so many unfinished craft projects around the house and garden, and I often start a new one before I've finished the other – especially if I hit a problem or a snag that's annoying to fix.

*5. Often has difficulty organising tasks and activities.*

The official explanation for this point is difficulty managing sequential tasks; difficulty keeping materials and belongings in order; messy, disorganised work; poor time management; and failing to meet deadlines. Or you could just put a photo of my face here to illustrate this one.

*6. Often avoids, dislikes, or is reluctant to engage in tasks that require sustained mental effort.*

When an ADHD brain has to do something unpleasant or inconvenient, it procrastinates or tries to palm it off. Sustained mental effort isn't necessarily an intellectual endeavour. For me, it's things like driving somewhere unfamiliar to find a place I've never been. Or, being asked to source something and not knowing who to phone. I get stuck when I'm not sure what the next step is, and so I avoid those tasks.

*7. Often loses things necessary for tasks or activities*

Some with this type of ADHD might for example, hypothetically, leave their phone charger at the beach cottage they went to last week, and also might have, just as an example, lost the application form for their kid's sports club, and also may or may not know where her credit card is, because she put it in her pocket a few days ago when she went for a walk. Hypothetically, of course.

*8. Is often easily distracted by external stimuli.*

For me, it's ambient sound. I cannot NOT hear background music. If I'm in a restaurant and I hate the song playing in the background, I literally have to stop speaking and wait for it to be done. I'll stop mid-sentence if a song I like comes on. If we're in the car and the radio is on while one of the boys is talking to me, I feel like my brain will explode and I cannot create a sentence. For the ADHD brain, this can also show up in having completely unrelated thoughts to what is going on externally around them.

*9. Is often forgetful in daily activities*

Returning calls, replying to emails, answering text messages – we just forget. My poor kids will ask me to buy them something for a school project and I will forget so many times.

## COMBINED TYPE

While the Hyperactive-Impulsive Type is mostly marked by hyperactivity and impulsivity, and the Inattentive Type is mostly marked by poor attention regulation, the Combined type where both inattention and hyperactivity/impulsivity are all present.

A diagnosis of Combined Type ADHD will be made if the symptoms have been present for at least 6 months, with quite a few being present before the age of 12 – even if they weren't diagnosed then.

The symptoms also need to be noticeable in more than one environment like school, work or home, and need to be obviously impacting the person's potential.

***

Should you recognise these symptoms in yourself or in others, please be motivated to take the next step towards health and support. ADHD is often diagnosed in conjunction with other factors, and symptoms can have other causes. Nothing here replaces talking with your healthcare professional to assess your condition and determine the need for a treatment plan appropriate for you.

To learn more about ADHD, I recommend www.additudemag.com as a reliable, well-researched, easy to navigate place to start.

Finally, if you think you or someone you know might be living with undiagnosed ADHD, please reach out to a mental health professional, psychiatrist or doctor with a special interest in ADHD.

***

# THANK YOU

To all of my families:
the Bassons, van Straatens, van Smylys,
Jorgensons, Grobbelaars and Callaghans.
I'm so grateful for my family by love and by law.

To my mom, Christine:
for editing my work meticulously and objectively.

To Jordan:
for the beautiful cover, artwork and illustrations, as well as your patience with me.

To Ashleigh:
for the gorgeous book layout and generous advice.

For your unique and faithful friendships:
Christie, Deb, Kath, Liesel, Michele, Nikki and Tory.

For your wisdom on writing:
Matt, Aaron, Catherine, Nicola and Kerry.

Printed in Great Britain
by Amazon

86387225R00116